1 & 2 Corinthians
Finding Your Unique Place in God's Plan

Bruce BICKEL
&
Stan JANTZ

HARVEST HOUSE PUBLISHERS

EUGENE, OREGON

Unless otherwise indicated, all Scripture quotations are taken from the *Holy Bible*, New Living Translation, copyright ©1996. Used by permission of Tyndale House Publishers, Inc., Wheaton, IL 60189 USA. All rights reserved.

Verses marked NIV are taken from the HOLY BIBLE, NEW INTERNATIONAL VERSION®. NIV®. Copyright©1973, 1978, 1984 by the International Bible Society. Used by permission of Zondervan. All rights reserved.

Verses marked KJV are taken from the King James Version of the Bible.

Cover by Left Coast Design, Portland, Oregon

Cover photo © Steve Terrill, Portland, Oregon, www.terrillphoto.com

CHRISTIANITY 101 is a registered trademark of The Hawkins Children's LLC. Harvest House Publishers, Inc., is the exclusive licensee of the federally registered trademark CHRISTIANITY 101.

1 & 2 CORINTHIANS: FINDING YOUR UNIQUE PLACE IN GOD'S PLAN
Copyright © 2004 by Bruce Bickel and Stan Jantz
Published by Harvest House Publishers
Eugene, Oregon 97402
www.harvesthousepublishers.com

Library of Congress Cataloging-in-Publication Data
Bickel, Bruce, 1952–
    1 & 2 Corinthians: finding your unique place in God's plan / Bruce Bickel and Stan Jantz.
        p. cm.—(Christianity 101)
    ISBN 0-7369-0938-9 (pbk.)
    1. Bible. N.T. Corinthians—Commentaries. I. Title: 1 and 2 Corinthians. II. Title: First and Second Corinthians. III. Jantz, Stan, 1952– IV. Title. V. Series.
    BS2675.53.B53 2004
    227'.207—dc22   2004006096

Printed in the United States of America

04   05   06   07   08   09   10   11   / DP-CF /   10   9   8   7   6   5   4   3   2   1

Contents

A Note from the Authors

*Y*ou may have selected this specific Bible study on 1 and 2 Corinthians for many reasons:

- Maybe you are studying your way through the Bible, covering all 66 books from beginning to end. You started with Genesis and have gotten as far as 1 Corinthians. (Congratulations. Forty-five books down, only 21 left to go.)

- Maybe you are intrigued by some particular passage in Paul's letters to the Corinthian Christians. Perhaps you're drawn to the "Love Chapter"—1 Corinthians 13. Or maybe you are curious about Paul's description of spiritual gifts or his teachings on marriage, divorce, and remarriage.

- You might be in a Bible study group and someone else picked the topic. Maybe the group had a few dissenters, but you went along with the leader's choice because you didn't want to be perceived as contentious. (You'll be looking very spiritual when we get to the passage about the importance of Christian unity.)

Whatever your reason for selecting this study, we think you'll end up learning more than you expected. That's what happened to us as we set out to write this Bible study. We anticipated learning some deep truths about God and the Christian life, and we expected to gain insights about the Christian faith. We got all of that. But the added—and unexpected—bonus was that we finished our study with a greater sense of how we fit into God's plan and how He has uniquely equipped each of us for the roles He has for us. We are convinced that 1 and 2 Corinthians will help you find your unique place in God's plan too.

Learning from the Mistakes of Others

There are two ways that you can learn about changing your behavior:

- *The hard way:* You can make a mistake yourself and get chewed out for it.

- *The easy way:* Other people make the mistakes, and you learn from overhearing the reprimands that they receive.

You've no doubt already experienced this phenomenon. Maybe your parent scolded your sibling, or a coach yelled at your teammate, or your boss chastised one of your coworkers. We'll guess that in each instance you thought, *I'm glad it's not me, and I now know how to act in the future.*

Welcome to the underlying principle for studying the books of 1 and 2 Corinthians. As we'll explain in more detail in chapter 1, the Christians in Corinth were a messed-up group. They were immoral (and arrogant about it). They were fighting among themselves and easily swayed by false teachers. Paul wrote his letters to the Christians in Corinth to set them straight. He doesn't coddle them. If fact, he is brutally honest about their spiritual immaturity. His letters are very direct about the specific changes they need to make in their lives if they are to grow and mature spiritually.

Paul never imagined that you would be studying his Corinthian letters about 2000 years after he wrote them. So he wasn't intending to make his letters a general treatise about the practical aspects of the Christian faith. Rather, he was writing to address the specific problems of the Corinthian Christians. But 1 and 2 Corinthians can be poignantly relevant to you if you apply what Paul is saying to your own life. Though he isn't lecturing you directly, you can gain great insight about your own faith by reading Paul's instruction to the Corinthians on subjects like these:

- getting along with other Christians
- living in an immoral culture
- moving beyond a religion focused on regulations to a faith based on a relationship with Christ
- understanding what truly worshipping God means
- discovering how God has specifically equipped you to minister to others

When you apply these principles to your life, you'll begin to realize your unique and essential role in God's plan. Imagine learning all of that, and you weren't even the one who got in trouble.

Christianity 101 Series

This Bible study is part of the Christianity 101 series that includes other Bible studies and resource books (such as *Knowing the Bible 101* and *Knowing God 101*). All of these books are designed to present the truth about God in a manner that is correct, clear, and casual. We intend the Bible studies to give you additional background information (as you'll find in a commentary but not as technical), along with questions that encourage you to apply what you have studied to your specific life circumstances.

As a participant in this Bible study, you're invited to log onto www.Christianity101online.com. There you will find additional resources, information, and study questions that may be helpful in your study of 1 and 2 Corinthians. Look for pages on that website for each of the books in the Christianity 101 series. You can also use the website to e-mail to us any questions you have about what you have studied. Look at the end of this book for more information about these online features.

Alone or in a Group

We've designed this Bible study for individuals as well as groups. So you can work through this book as part of a personal daily devotional plan or as part of a weekly study group. The questions at the end of each chapter are designed for personal reflection as well as group discussion.

We don't usually print the verses we are discussing. That is what your Bible is for. We suggest that you read the Bible passage first and then read through the chapter in this book. Then, reread the Bible passage for a second time. (Hey, these are short passages we are talking about, so you'll still have time for eating and sleeping.) We think you'll be surprised at how much better you understand that passage when you read it the second time.

Discovering How and Where You Fit In

Because you are serious enough about your Christian faith to be studying the Bible, we are confident that you want to please God. We have no doubt that you want to grow in your faith, and we're glad that you want to be all God intends for you. In 1 and 2 Corinthians, you will find a foundation for that kind of spiritual maturity.

As we've written this book, we've been praying that God will guide our words to clearly communicate how Paul's instruction to the Corinthians can help you discover your unique place in God's plan. But you should also know that we've been praying for you too. Really. We know that when you discover how and where you fit into God's plan, and when you realize how He has uniquely equipped you for His purposes, you will be overwhelmed with a tremendous sense of His presence in your life.

This was Paul's hope for the Christians in Corinth:

> *And as the Spirit of the Lord works within us, we become more and more like him and reflect his glory even more* (2 Corinthians 3:18).

That is our prayer for you.

Chapter 1

Much has been written about the sexual
mores of Corinth.... What seems more
significant is the general tone of the city: its
drive and enthusiasm, its focus on success
and personal achievement. As we look into
the epistle which Paul wrote to his "problem
congregation" there, we quickly sense that
these qualities have infected the church, and
are reflected in the drive of its members to
establish their own prestige within the fellowship of faith. Surely in our own society
we value the traits of hard work, enthusiasm, and commitment to personal success
that marked the men and women of Corinth.
And yet those very traits, as we will see, may
be destructive to the unity we must learn to
develop as we live together as members of
the one body of our Lord Jesus Christ.

Lawrence O. Richards

A More Spiritual Time and Place?

Let's face it. It is not easy being a Christian in our contemporary culture. We're living in a society that continually bombards our senses with secular influences that promote success, materialism, and sex. No wonder we have a difficult time deciding where we fit in God's plan. We're living in an age when our Christian values are out of sync with the rest of the world. And life isn't always easier within our churches. Sometimes getting along with other Christians can be our greatest challenge (and disappointment).

Have you ever envied those first-century Christians? Oh sure, they had the hardships of no air conditioning and no flush toilets when they gathered for worship. And let's not forget about the Roman persecution that included tossing Christians into the lion-filled arena. But at least those first-century Christians didn't have to deal with the rampant immorality of our X-rated world, and at least they were in close, intimate friendship with their fellow believers. (After all, doesn't persecution facilitate bonding relationships?)

Well, you can stop dreaming of the "good ol' days" of A.D. 50. As you are about to find out, those times weren't so conducive for nurturing the Christian faith. The Corinthian believers' city was morally perverted and their relationships in the church were contentious. In fact, their situation was a lot like ours is today. That's why Paul's advice to them is so relevant to us.

Corinthians:
Christians in Need of Guidance

What's Ahead

- Corinth: City at a Crossroads

- The Corinthian Church: Christians at Cross-Purposes

- One Letter, Two Letters, Three Letters, Four?

What do you get when you mix spiritually imma-ture Christians with a culture that is extrava-gant, immoral, superficial, and status-conscious? You get the Corinthian Christians. These believers, ignoring the development of their faith, got caught up in their city's quest for prestige, wealth, and all the accompanying depravity. If anyone could come to the spiritual rescue of these Christians in crisis, you've got to believe that Paul—the super missionary to the Gentile world—was the man for the job. Well, as you'll soon see, the Corinthians were perhaps Paul's greatest challenge.

Corinth: City at a Crossroads

Let's start our study with the revival and rebuilding of Corinth that began in 44 B.C., when Julius Caesar established a Roman colony there. As a Roman city-state in Greece, Corinth had great political significance. Within the following century, it grew to a city of great cultural and commercial prominence. By the middle of the first-century A.D., Corinth had achieved the following distinctions:

- It had a population of approximately 700,000 (perhaps two-thirds of which were slaves).

- It was the site of the Roman government for the province of Achaia (representing most of Greece). Only Rome had more political significance than Corinth.

- For cultural events, it had an indoor theatre that seated 3000.

- For outdoor sporting events, it had a 20,000-seat coliseum.

- Its invitational sporting events were second only to the Olympics in Athens.

But Corinth had a dark, immoral side. Surprisingly, the Corinth Chamber of Commerce wasn't embarrassed about it. Just the contrary. The immorality of Corinth was one of the city's most publicized attractions. In earlier years, it had maintained one of the world's largest temples as a place to worship Aphrodite, the Greek goddess of love. The temple employed more than 1000 prostitutes who encouraged local citizens and visitors in all sorts of debauchery. This reputation—and influence—remained and flourished through the first century.

Corinth was the cosmopolitan center of the world, literally as well as figuratively. The geography of eastern Greece is the reason for its political, social, commercial, and immoral significance. Corinth was at the center of a narrow isthmus (only four miles wide) that connected all of Europe to the southern part of Greece (the region known as Achaia). Like the center of an hourglass, everything passed through Corinth regardless of which direction it traveled. If you were traveling north to south, or vice versa, you went through Corinth. And if you were traveling by ship from the east to the west, or vice versa, you probably wanted to avoid the dangerous waters at the southern tip of Greece, so you docked at the seaport at Corinth and boarded a different ship at the docks on the other side of the city. Thus, it became one of the leading cosmopolitan centers of the world (and it was exposed to all of the philosophies and perversions that the world had to offer).

The Corinthian Church: Christians at Cross-Purposes

Perhaps more than any other of the fledgling Christian churches of the first century, the Corinthian church couldn't shake the secular influences of its city. But the outside forces weren't what spiritually crippled the Corinthian Christians. The problem with the church in Corinth was with the *Christians* in Corinth. They were so enamored with the secular lifestyle that they didn't want to give it up. They lived in a culture that emphasized self-importance, ambition, and status. That's the mind-set they had before they were Christians, and they brought those same feelings into their church.

The Corinthian Christians suffered from superiority schizophrenia. Their church was divided into groups, each group claiming that it was more "spiritual" than the others.

- Some groups based their claim of superiority on the human leader that they followed.

- Others claimed to be spiritually superior because they didn't engage in sexual immorality as others did.

- Some claimed that they held the spiritual top spot because they even refrained from sexual relations with their spouses.

- Another group took pride in the fact that its members didn't eat meat that had been used in pagan idol worship.

- One group thought it deserved spiritual high marks because its members held high positions in society.

- Some wanted to impose a hierarchy of spiritual gifts (putting their gift of "tongues" at the top of the list).

These Christians were so self-centered that they had lost sight of what God wanted them to become.

$\mathcal{Q}$ualified for the $\mathcal{J}$ob

We'll cover more of Paul's credentials later. For now, let's just introduce him as the best known of the first-century missionaries who brought the Gospel message to the Gentile (non-Jewish) population. Paul was particularly well suited for the challenges of the Corinthian church. He had a résumé that would be important to the Corinthians:

- He was an intellectual and well educated.

- He was well traveled and familiar with the variety of ethnic and cultural influences in Corinth.

- He had Roman citizenship (because his father was born a Roman citizen).

On the other hand, many of the Corinthians found some things about Paul objectionable. For instance, while in Corinth, he earned his living in the lowly occupation of a tent maker (which certainly didn't impress the status-conscious Corinthians). And regarding oratory skills, Paul wasn't the best public speaker (which gave the Corinthians something else to criticize).

But his combination of strength and weakness was exactly what the Corinthians needed. His experiences allowed him to understand the basis for their aberrant beliefs, and his weaknesses illustrated how God can work in and through a believer.

One Letter, Two Letters, Three Letters, Four?

If you were asked how many letters Paul wrote to the Christians at the church in Corinth, you'd probably answer two. (After all, this is a Bible study on 1 and 2 Corinthians, so the answer seems obvious, doesn't it?) Well, maybe you shouldn't be so quick to respond.

A Visit Followed by a Letter

Paul probably arrived in Corinth for the first time in A.D. 51. (He was on his second of three missionary journeys, and he had just finished ministering in Athens.) He established a church in Corinth and stayed there for approximately 18 months.

Sometime after his departure from Corinth, Paul apparently wrote a letter to the Corinthians. This letter actually preceded our letter of 1 Corinthians. Paul refers to this earlier letter in 1 Corinthians 5:9 when he says,

"When I wrote to you before, I told you.... " This first letter is not part of the Bible, and its contents are unknown.

Paul journeyed on to Ephesus and visited the church in Jerusalem before returning to his home at Antioch. Before long, he set off on his third missionary journey, starting with visits in Galatia and Phrygia and then moving on to Ephesus, where he stayed for almost three years.

A Troubling Report Prompts 1 Corinthians

While Paul was still in Ephesus, a delegation of believers from the Corinthian church met with Paul. They reported to him the disastrous state of their church. Although four or five years had passed since he had been with them, Paul felt a spiritual responsibility for this young church. He responded to the crisis by writing a letter to the church (which is known as 1 Corinthians).

First Corinthians emphasizes the importance of Christian unity. But that's not all. Paul also punctured overinflated spiritual egos by exposing their erroneous views of certain doctrines and practices.

Try to Find Yourself

As you read through the Corinthian letters, try to find yourself. Are you guilty of spiritual arrogance? Do you think you are spiritually superior to others because of something you do (or something you refrain from doing)? Take Paul's instruction to heart and make some changes in the way you live and the way you think about yourself and others. You'll never find your place in God's plan until you have the correct perspective of yourself and others.

A Letter Between the Pages

Your Bible probably doesn't have any blank pages between 1 and 2 Corinthians. One letter immediately follows the next. But a lot actually happened in the three-year interlude between these two letters. Here is what evidently occurred:

- Upon writing 1 Corinthians while he was in Ephesus, Paul dispatched Timothy to deliver his letter and help with some of the corrective efforts (1 Corinthians 4:17).

- To some extent at least, the Christians in Corinth cleaned up their spiritual lives after reading 1 Corinthians.

- But not everything improved, and some things got worse. Things deteriorated so much that Timothy felt compelled to leave Corinth and bring a personal report to Paul in Ephesus.

- So Paul interrupted his planned missionary itinerary and made an emergency visit to Corinth. This second visit to the city apparently didn't go well. It was a painful experience for both Paul and the Corinthians (see 2 Corinthians 2:1; 12:14).

- Upon returning back to Ephesus, Paul shot off another letter to the Corinthians. It must have been both emotional and severe. Titus took the letter back to Corinth, and he stayed in the city to minister on Paul's behalf. (Unfortunately, this letter isn't included in the Bible. Scholars refer to it as the "lost letter" to the Corinthians. Paul refers to it in 2 Corinthians 7:5-16.)

- Apparently, the "lost letter" hit a nerve, and the Corinthians responded positively to it. Titus brought the good news to Paul, who by this time had continued his missionary trip into Macedonia. But Titus also brought some bad news about renegade missionaries who had infiltrated the Corinthian church and were challenging Paul's credentials as an apostle.

Another Troubling Report Prompts 2 Corinthians (and a Visit)

When Paul got the "good news and bad news" from Titus, he wrote another letter. This is the letter known as 2 Corinthians (although it appears to be the fourth letter in the chronology). Paul sent Titus back with the letter while Paul concluded his ministry in Macedonia and made plans for a third visit to Corinth.

The themes of 2 Corinthians are related to Paul's reconciliation to the Corinthians: salving any hurt feelings with the Corinthians, resolving differences with those who opposed him, and encouraging reconciliation between the church members themselves. Most importantly, Paul wanted the Corinthian Christians to rekindle their love of Christ.

In what may have been A.D. 56–57, Paul made this third visit to Corinth about one year after writing 2 Corinthians (see Acts 20:2-3). Apparently the conciliatory tone of 2 Corinthians paved the way for a harmonious visit. He stayed there for three months (during which time he wrote or completed his letter to the Romans, which gives no hint of any continuing problems in Corinth).

It's a $\mathcal{R}$elationship, $\mathcal{N}$ot a $\mathcal{R}$eligion

Here's what we suggest as your homework assignment for this chapter. Speed-read your way through 1 and 2 Corinthians. Don't worry if some of it seems confusing; we'll get to those difficult passages in subsequent chapters. On this first reading, your task is to get a sense of the one thing that Paul makes abundantly clear: Christianity is not about a religion of rules and regulations. It is all about a faith in Christ based on a relationship with Him. A proper relationship with Christ will put the rest of your life in order, including your individual relationships with other people. You've got to comprehend the relational aspects of the Christian life. Only then can you begin to realize your unique role in God's plan and His purposes for your life.

■ ■ ■

Study the Word

1. Paul had a spectacular conversion experience. Read about it in Acts 9:1-31. Do you think his past history (as a persecutor of Christians) and his dramatic conversion made him more tolerant or less tolerant of the immature Christian behavior he encountered in Corinth?

2. Read Acts 18:1-17 for a brief overview of Paul's first visit to Corinth. Why do you think Paul began his ministry there by preaching to the Jews in the synagogue?

3. As you read through these two letters, take note of the different emotions and approaches that Paul uses with his readers. Sometimes he is confrontational, other times he is conciliatory, occasionally he is sarcastic. How would you describe his tone in these verses: 1 Corinthians 3:1; 5:1-2; 6:7; and 11:17? What about 2 Corinthians 7:2 and 10:1-2? And why does he change his style?

4. In 1 Corinthians, Paul answers the Corinthians' questions about Christian behavior, lifestyle, and doctrine. If you could ask Paul about such matters, what would your questions be?

5. If Paul were writing a letter to you, what would be some of the issues he would ask you to deal with in your spiritual life?

Chapter 2

The Corinthian Christians had allowed divisions over human philosophies to come into the church. They had chosen certain religious leaders to gather around, and so now they were divided into factions.... The deep issues of God and the life of the Spirit cannot be settled by a popularity contest or by philosophical debate. They can only be settled by the Word of God. That is still true today. The church will never solve its problems as long as it constantly pursues this writer and that teacher, this pastor or that speaker.... The apostle Paul answers the factions and divisions in Corinth by confronting the Corinthian church with the word of the cross—the word that presents the cross of Christ as the instrument by which God cuts off all human wisdom, not as being worthless in its own narrow realm, but as being useless in solving the major problems of human beings.

Ray C. Stedman

One-Half of a Conversation

In some of his other letters, Paul moves slowly and gently into the discussion of sensitive subjects. Not with the Corinthians. After just a few verses of the traditional greeting, he jumps right into his assessment of their problems.

Don't be surprised by Paul's bluntness. Remember, this wasn't his first letter to them. With 1 Corinthians, he is actually continuing an earlier dialogue with the Corinthian Christians. Also, remember that you're just reading one-half of the conversation. Think of it as if you were listening while someone near you was on the phone. You're only hearing Paul's comments, and you've got to imagine what was said to him that prompted his comments. (Don't worry. He's so blunt that you'll have no trouble filling in the blanks.)

Here's another tip to understanding the context. Paul probably didn't take a long, drawn-out, and methodical approach to writing and rewriting versions of this letter. You'll see that it is too intense for such a tranquil method. He probably paced back and forth in a room, shouting out his inspirations from the Holy Spirit, while some assistant feverishly transcribed what he said.

You may only be reading one side of a conversation, but you'll be getting plenty to think about.

You've Got to Change the Way You Think

1 Corinthians 1–2

*I*n these first two chapters of 1 Corinthians, Paul severely abbreviates the pleasantries and quickly gets down to the problem of divisiveness in the church. But factions and divisions are merely the readily apparent, external symptoms of a more serious underlying problem: The Corinthians aren't thinking like Christians.

Greetings with a Subtext (1:1-9)

The customary salutation of the first century included the name of the author, the names of the intended recipients, and a blessing. Paul includes each of those elements in the opening verses of 1 Corinthians, but don't miss the nuances:

- *The author:* "Paul, chosen by the will of God to be an apostle" (1:1). Some people in Corinth challenged Paul's spiritual authority. Here he makes clear that his apostleship is due to God's plan, not his own scheming. If God considers him an apostle, who can argue the point? (Although he wasn't a coauthor of the letter, Paul mentions Sosthenes here. He may have been one of Paul's attendants who was known to the Corinthians and wanted to convey his greetings to them.)

- *The recipients:* "To the church of God in Corinth" (1:2). Okay, it is no surprise that this letter is written to the Corinthian church. But Paul doesn't say it that way. It is written to *God's church* in Corinth. Paul is politely reminding them: "Hey, your church isn't about you and what you want or what makes you happy. The church is all about God." (Churches would have far fewer squabbles if people remembered this principle.) And the Christians there were "called by God to be his own holy people." That doesn't mean God expected them to be perfect or sinless. In this context, "holy" refers to being set apart for service to God.

- *The blessing:* "Grace and peace" (1:3). This has much more meaning than the typical "God bless you" that you might utter when someone sneezes. *Grace* refers to the gift of salvation that God gives to us even though we don't deserve it. *Peace* doesn't mean an absence of problems. It implies the spiritual strength to transcend the emotional turmoil of either prosperity or adversity. Note the source of this grace and peace.

In verses 4-9, Paul expresses words of thanks to God. This follows his custom in other letters where he mentions his thankfulness for certain features of his readers' spiritual lives. But in this passage, you won't find that he says anything complimentary about the Corinthians themselves. Instead, he expresses gratitude for what God has done for them. Thus, the Corinthians can't take credit.

- *God* gave them spiritual gifts.

- *God* will keep them spiritually strong.

- *God* invited them into a relationship with Christ.

*G*ot *P*urpose?

If you're looking for God's plan for your life, these nine verses give you some important guidance. Notice that Paul felt "chosen" or *called* by God to be an apostle. You can find a similar sense of purpose in your life. That process begins with understanding that Christ has made you holy and set apart for service to Him. And God has given you the spiritual gifts and talents that you'll be using in those sacred endeavors.

Divisive Divisions (1:10-17)

Although several years had passed since his last visit to Corinth, Paul knew exactly what was happening there. He had received up-to-date reports by messengers from the church, such as Stephanas, Fortunatus, Achaicus (16:17), and members of Chloe's household (1:11). From these reports, Paul knew that some of the Corinthians were creating splits within their church. Sometimes the people of a church are divided in a way that is acceptable (such as when one group goes to an early Sunday morning "traditional" service and another group goes to a later "contemporary" service). But the divisions in Corinth weren't acceptable. These Christians were arguing with each other—and not even about doctrines of the Christian faith. People were alienating themselves from each other in a popularity contest. In a kind of Christian celebrity sweepstakes, some people were choosing sides behind Paul. Others were claiming allegiance to different leaders:

- *Apollos* was a Jew from Alexandria, Egypt, who visited Corinth. Many people were attracted to his knowledge of the Scriptures and his eloquence (Acts 18:24).

- *Peter* (also known as Cephas in Aramaic) was one of the 12 disciples and a leader in the church in Jerusalem. He had been a member of Christ's inner circle.

- One faction in Corinth was evidently pridefully boasting that they followed *Christ* alone.

Such loyalties to individual leaders were driving wedges between the believers. Paul implored them to stop their arguing and pursue harmony in their fellowship. The friction from these petty arguments was bad enough in itself (because it violated God's intent for unity in the church), but another effect was even more disastrous: The Corinthians were focusing more on the *messenger* than the *message*. Their fixation with communication skills had obscured the importance of the cross of Christ. That's why Paul says he avoided clever speeches and high-sounding ideas in the sermons he preached to them. He didn't want the presentation to detract in any manner from the power of the Gospel.

$\mathcal{N}$ote the $\mathcal{S}$arcasm

The well-educated Corinthian Christians would have quickly noticed the sarcasm in Paul's rhetorical questions (1:12-13): Can Christ be divided? Was I crucified for you? Were you baptized in the name of Paul? To each one, the obvious answer was a resounding "Of course not!"

Spiritual Foolishness Trumps Worldly Wisdom (1:18–2:5)

The Corinthians were trying to live out the Christian faith while they clung to the mind-set of their secular culture, but they weren't having much success. Their society admired intellectualism and despised the seemingly silly, naïve beliefs of Christianity.

The beliefs of Christianity have always been out of sync with human understanding. Humanity, impressed with its own intelligence, can't think big enough to grasp the simplicity of God's plan. Nothing brought out this disparity of thought in the first century more than the crucifixion.

- The Jews couldn't comprehend that Jesus was the Messiah because He was crucified. They thought that God would establish His kingdom through a political revolution; they didn't realize that He desired an inward transformation of the heart. They expected their Messiah to be a conquering hero, not a suffering servant. Consequently, the crucifixion of Christ was a "stumbling block" to understanding God's wisdom (Isaiah 8:14; Romans 9:33; 1 Peter 2:8).

- Like the Jews, the Greeks couldn't believe that a "Savior" of the world would be crucified. They knew that crucifixion was a penalty imposed by the Roman government for only the vilest criminals. To the Greek way of thinking, supposing that any good person would be crucified was sheer "foolishness."

Paul uses two personal examples to remind the Corinthians that God uses apparently foolish things to impress His truth upon those who arrogantly think they are wise.

- *Paul reminds the Corinthians of their own simplicity.* Some in the Corinthian church had attained social status, but most were lowly members of society. Paul says that "few of you were wise in the world's eyes, or powerful, or wealthy when God called you" (1:26). He was pointing out that they lacked intellectual, political, or social qualifications, yet God chose them as His instruments to spread the Gospel message in Corinth.

- *Paul reminds the Corinthians of his simplistic preaching.* Being so captivated by the appeal of intellectual and philosophical wisdom, the Corinthian believers may have forgotten what attracted them to the Gospel message in the first place. Paul reminds them that he did not use "lofty words and brilliant ideas." He intentionally stayed away from a dynamic approach that would draw attention to him. He came to them very humbly with a message that was empowered by the Holy Spirit rather than by human oratorical skills: "I did this so that you might trust the power of God rather than human wisdom" (2:5).

What Kind of Wisdom Is Paul Talking About?

The verses you're reading are filled with references to God's wisdom. Paul uses this term in a much broader sense than the type of wisdom that fills the pages of Proverbs: "These proverbs will make the simpleminded clever. They will give knowledge and purpose to young people. Let those who are wise listen to these proverbs and become wiser" (Proverbs 1:4-5).

Paul's use of the term *wisdom* goes beyond mere knowledge, insight, and good judgment. In Paul's lexicon, *wisdom* refers to God's spiritual paradigm. It encompasses God's entire concept of salvation. Thus, human wisdom is based on our limited reality. In contrast, God's wisdom encompasses not only our physical realities but also the entirety of the spiritual realm.

Start Thinking the Way God Thinks (2:6-16)

Paul was a proponent of transformational thinking. The Corinthians weren't the only ones who were stuck in the mind-set of their culture and needed to change their perspective. Paul said the same thing to the Christians in Rome:

> *Don't copy the behavior and customs of this world, but let God transform you into a new person by changing the way you think. Then you will know what God wants you to do* (Romans 12:2).

You must start thinking the way God thinks if you're ever going to understand His plan for your life. But shifting your thinking patterns from "worldly wisdom" to "godly wisdom" doesn't come naturally. You need transformational thinking that comes to you supernaturally, and that is just what God provides.

God's Got a Secret

Are you curious about Paul's assessment of the spiritual maturity of the Corinthians? Well, he didn't keep it a secret. After explaining that he came to them with plain and simple preaching (2:4), he says that he can delve into deeper wisdom only when he is with "mature Christians" (2:6). We don't think he was cruelly disrespecting the Corinthians, but he does seem to be making a point: God's wisdom is wasted on people who aren't spiritually mature enough to handle it.

Paul mentions that God's wisdom was a secret in "former times" (before Christ). Until the crucifixion and resurrection of Christ, the Jews were awaiting a Messiah, but they expected this coming Savior to be a leader who would save them from political and economic oppression. No one ever conceived that God's plan would encompass the path to Calvary. Even today, most people are at a loss to comprehend God's eternal plan and how the death of Jesus figures into it.

You Can Know What God Is Thinking

But God doesn't keep His wisdom secret from those who are fully devoted followers of Christ. In a rational explanation in 2:10-12, Paul explains the sequence by which God makes His truth available to us:

- No one can know God's own thoughts except His Spirit.

- God has given His Spirit to every Christian.

- The Spirit reveals God's thoughts to us.

We can never know all that God knows. We will never fully comprehend all that He is. But the Holy Spirit gives us insights into His truth and wisdom (which would otherwise seem as foolishness to us). Thus, in a very real sense, we can know some of the thoughts of God. And on this profound note, Paul concludes 1 Corinthians 2 with the statement that we can understand the wisdom of God because "we have the mind of Christ" (2:16).

$\mathcal{T}$hink $\mathcal{A}$bout $\mathcal{T}$his

You can only begin to know what God has in mind for you when you begin to have His mind.

$\mathcal{S}$tudy the $\mathcal{W}$ord

1. Compare 1 Corinthians 1:4-9 with the "thanksgiving" portion of Paul's salutation in Philippians 1:3-11. What are the differences in Paul's tone? Can you think of an explanation for these differences?

2. How do people happen to choose a "favorite" minister? What are the dangers of attaching your allegiance to one particular Christian leader? What should ministers do to avoid this problem? How did Paul handle it?

3. How would Paul define human wisdom? What would be his description of God's wisdom?

4. Why does God's wisdom seem foolish to those who are not Christians?

5. How would you respond to someone who accused you of blasphemy for saying that you had "the mind of Christ"?

Chapter 3

The fact that Paul refers to the Corinthians as being "in Christ" shows they're saved. But instead of moving on to maturity, they remained spiritually stunted. Why? Because they were mixing the world and the Word. They came to church on Sunday and took in the studies. They clapped their hands in worship and even put money in the offering. But on Monday they were out in the world again. Consequently, they were neither fish nor fowl, miserable because they had too much of the world in them to really enjoy the Lord, yet too much of the Lord in them to really enjoy the world.

Jon Courson

Right Thinking Leads to Right Living

Being a Christian—and living like one—is serious business. It includes principles that we can't gloss over or cover quickly. That's why Paul dwells on the subject of what it means to *think* like a Christian.

After having explained the difference between worldly thinking and godly wisdom (in 1 Corinthians 1 and 2), Paul moves logically to the next step: how Christian thinking affects Christian living. He'll eventually get into some very practical topics (such as immorality, disagreements, and marriage and divorce). But he's not ready to go there just yet. First he wants to apply the principles of Christian thinking to the heart of the Christian life.

If you are serious about finding your unique place in God's grand design, 1 Corinthians 3 and 4 will provide you with some invaluable guidelines.

Building upon a
Spiritual Foundation

1 Corinthians 3–4

*P*aul has already talked about rancor that existed in the Corinthian church because the members were taking sides behind their favorite leaders. Now he uses that situation to springboard into a discussion of spiritual immaturity. The Corinthians needed instruction about spiritual growth. So do we all. God's great plans for each of us assume that we'll be growing beyond spiritual infancy.

Baby Christians That Aren't So Cute (3:1-4)

Paul looks back with fondness at his early ministry in Corinth. The people were brand-new converts to the

Christian faith. They were baby Christians. Just as parents feed real infants milk and not solid food for a while, Paul had to feed the Corinthians "milk" instead of heavy theological truths. They needed him to puree what he preached to them so they could digest it. That's the way people are when they experience spiritual rebirth. And this is a good thing.

But staying that way is a bad thing. And the Corinthian Christians stayed immature in their faith. Paul is critical that they have failed to develop as Christians. He is still forced to keep his lessons simple because they are incapable of eating the "solid food" of Scripture.

Paul's basis for evaluating the Corinthians' spiritual maturity (or lack thereof) is rather interesting. He says they are immature Christians because they are still "controlled by [their] sinful desires." As we'll see in later chapters, this includes immorality and other sexual excesses, but carnality doesn't always involve sensual behavior. In fact, in this passage Paul identifies their worldly conduct as their jealousy and quarreling with each other. Their contentious relationships with other Christians simply don't reflect the character of Christ.

A Spiritual Growth Chart

Do you ever wonder how you would measure up on a spiritual growth chart? We have no single objective standard, but 1 Corinthians 3:3 gives some guidance. A person's relationship with God is revealed by that person's relationships with other people. If your relationships with others, particularly other Christians, are filled with animosity, jealousy, or indifference, you might be registering at the "baby" end of the Christian growth chart. On the other hand, if you display the godly traits of love, respect, and service to your friends and others, you are definitely registering spiritual growth.

The Growing and Building Process (3:5-17)

Paul goes on to teach the Corinthians some principles regarding Christian ministry. He points out that a diversity of ministers labor in a common ministry. His comments are specifically directed at the Corinthians' proclivity to prefer one Christian leader over others. But his explanation is relevant to anyone who is serious about ministering for Christ: Without an understanding of these principles, any one of us is likely to think that we are more important than someone else who ministers in a different manner.

Paul recognizes different *kinds* of Christian ministries, but because ministers work "as a team with the same purpose," they all have the same *value*. Certainly Paul (who founded the church in Corinth) was different in style and approach than Apollos (who taught in the church after Paul left), but both of them were basically servants of Christ, "partners who belong to God." They were acting according to their God-given assignments.

An Agricultural Analogy

Paul uses an agricultural analogy to explain the cooperative effort of Christian ministry. If the Corinthian believers were crops, then Paul did the planting and Apollos did the watering. Each did the work God assigned to him, but neither of them could take credit for the growth of the crops. That was God's doing. Paul and Apollos were just the farmhands. God deserves all of the credit.

A Construction Analogy

The involvement of other Christian workers doesn't give anyone an excuse to slack off (to let the others pick up the slack). We are each responsible for our own assignments, and God will evaluate our efforts. Paul makes these points by using a construction analogy.

- Paul laid the foundation (the essential biblical teachings that brought the Corinthians to a saving knowledge and relationship with Christ).

- Others, such as Apollos, subsequently built on the foundation.

- But those who come later can't put down a new foundation. The foundation Paul laid (Jesus Christ) is already in place.

- The people who build upon the original foundation can either use quality building materials or junk. They can be skilled craftsmen or inferior laborers.

Apparently some inferior laborers were hanging out in the Corinthian church. Paul warns his readers by reminding them that the fellowship of believers is like the temple of God. They are the dwelling place of the Spirit of God, so they should be very careful about the people they allow to influence them. God will deal severely with "anyone who ruins this temple."

Judgment Day

Christians won't be judged at the Great White Throne judgment with unbelievers because God has already forgiven the sins of Christians (John 3:18; Romans 8:1). In 1 Corinthians 3:13, Paul is referring to the Judgment Seat of Christ (2 Corinthians 5:10 NIV), where God will evaluate the quality of our service to Him. Some things we do in life will count for eternity (what Paul refers to as "gold, silver, jewels"). Other selfish and frivolous efforts ("wood, hay, or straw" in Paul's terminology) will be considered by God as a waste of time.

If you're already a Christian, your salvation is assured, and you'll want to be building His Kingdom with quality materials if you intend to make a significant impact according to God's plan. The rewards you obtain at the Judgment Seat of Christ will be all you have to offer back to Christ. You won't want to be left empty-handed on that day.

Progressing Beyond Immaturity (3:18-23)

Instead of playing favorites within the church according to the standards of their pagan culture, the Corinthian Christians need to pursue unity in their fellowship based on spiritual wisdom. Paul gives three steps to moving out of their immaturity:

- *Stop fooling yourselves.* They considered themselves clever for exalting certain leaders. That might have been a popular approach in the society at large, but it was sheer foolishness within the church.

- *Stop boasting about leaders.* He earlier explained why. We overlook God when we look at the accomplishments of other people. Anything they do is only by the grace and power of God.

- *Realize that God has given you everything.* He encourages them to recognize that all things of God have been given to them. They don't need to worry about jealousies over which group has Paul, which group has Apollos, and which group has Peter. These men—and their talents—are God's gifts to the entire church. In fact, all aspects of the worldly and heavenly realm belong to all Christians because we all belong to God.

This Way to Maturity

An initial step out of spiritual immaturity is appreciation of the inheritance that we have as Christians. This is not just a lesson for the Corinthians. We need to learn it too.

And when you believed in Christ, he identified you as his own by giving you the Holy Spirit, whom he promised long ago. The Spirit is God's guarantee that he will give us everything he promised and that he has purchased us to be his own people. This is just one more reason for us to praise our glorious God (Ephesians 1:13-14).

It's a Tough Job If You Do It Right (4:1-13)

First Corinthians 4 wraps up Paul's discussion of divisions in the church. He gives the Corinthians an insider's view of what being a servant of Christ means, perhaps hoping that they'll have newfound respect for all Christians who minister in the church (instead of just picking a favorite and despising the others).

Three Evaluations (and the First Two Don't Count)

Your faithfulness to Christ may be evaluated on three levels:

- *Other people.* As you'll see, Paul is sensitive about what other people think about him (he gets fairly defensive later on). But he doesn't set his life's direction according to the opinions of others, so in this sense their opinion doesn't matter to him.

- *Your own opinion.* Your conscience is an indicator of your faithfulness, but it is not completely accurate. Paul didn't even trust his own judgment.

- *God.* The highest level—and the only one that matters—is God's evaluation. He will render the ultimate assessment of our effectiveness as stewards at the final day of judgment.

Since God's judgment is the only one that matters, we shouldn't be so quick to judge others. We shouldn't brag about some individuals and criticize other people.

It's Not All Fun and Games

Next Paul addresses the Corinthians' pride problem. In their spiritual immaturity, they were bragging about their own gifts. Paul reminds them that everything they have is from God. Then, to give them an accurate picture of Christian ministry, he contrasts his life with their situation. He uses a touch of sarcasm to point out their immaturity and the signs of his faithfulness. Their inflated opinion of themselves ends up looking a little ironic.

Their Opinion of Themselves	*Paul's Reality*
Royalty	Prisoner
Wise	Fool for Christ
Powerful and Influential	Weak
Socialites	Social Laughingstock

To give them an accurate picture of the cost of being a disciple of Christ, Paul offers a little glimpse of some of what he has endured: hunger and thirst, poverty and homelessness, beatings and imprisonment, and the list goes on.

Don't Miss It

If you are sincere about finding your place in God's plan, 1 Corinthians 4:2 should be underlined in your Bible. It says God's criterion for evaluating our service is faithfulness. Do you realize what this means? No other special abilities are prerequisites to serving God. It doesn't matter that we can't preach like Billy Graham or sing like Michael W. Smith. The talents and gifts that God gives us are not signs of spiritual superiority or inferiority. Neither are the assignments that He gives to us. All that matters is our faithfulness to Him as we use what He gives us and do what He asks us to do.

Father Knows Best (4:14-21)

Paul was hoping that a deeper understanding of Christian service would shock the Corinthians out of their spiritual arrogance and stop them from being so judgmental. He wasn't trying to lay a guilt trip on them, but he worried they might be stuck in a stage of spiritual infancy without his prodding.

As founder of their church, Paul was a spiritual father to the Corinthians. Most fathers have to say, "Do as I say," but their conduct doesn't match their words. But Paul was able to say, "Do as I do" (4:16). The degree of faithfulness in Christian service that he has outlined (4:10-13) is the standard he wants them to follow. To help in this process, he will send Timothy to Corinth. As one of Paul's protégés, Timothy would be able to encourage the Corinthians in their spiritual growth.

Paul also expresses his plan to make another visit to Corinth. This will give him a chance to confront some of his critics (who had become bold in their personal attacks on him, assuming he wouldn't return). He welcomes the opportunity to deal with these "big talkers" to see if they were acting in God's power or just out of selfish ambition.

Paul concludes this blunt commentary with a final challenge. He has said some tough words to the Corinthians. They bragged about their loyalty to Christ, so now he wants to know if it was all talk or whether they'll make the changes necessary to progress out of their spiritual immaturity. Their response will determine whether his next visit is as a proud father or as one who needs to administer some discipline.

◼ ◼ ◼

$\mathcal{S}$tudy the $\mathcal{W}$ord

1. What are some signs of spiritual immaturity? What should you do if you find some of these signs in your own life?

2. Explain how ministries can differ in style but have equal value.

3. What did you learn about judging others—and judging yourself—from studying this chapter?

4. Describe the Corinthians' immature view of Christian service. What would Paul say Christian service really is?

5. What is the significance of 1 Corinthians 4:2 if you are intent on finding out how you fit into God's plan?

Chapter 4

In sexual matters the heathen did not know the meaning of chastity. They took their pleasure when and where they wanted it. It was so hard for the Christian church to escape the infection. They were like a little island surrounded on every side by a sea of paganism; they had come so newly into Christianity; it was so difficult to unlearn the practices which generations of loose-living had made part of their lives; and yet if the Church was to be kept pure they must say a final good-bye to the old heathen ways.

William Barclay

How Could They Do Such Things?

What you are about to read in chapters 5 and 6 of 1 Corinthians might startle you. Paul makes reference to a particular sexual sin and a list of other perversions, but that's not what we think you'll find appalling. The shocking fact is that these things were happening in the church and that the Corinthians were self-righteously indignant about their spiritual liberties to engage in such conduct.

At the outset, we can easily be condescending and wonder, *How could those Corinthians do stuff like that? What could they have been thinking?*

But the challenge is for each of us to look at our own lives as we study this chapter. What aspects of society's lifestyle have we allowed to infect our thinking so we don't even see the horrible sin we're incubating within us?

The Corinthians weren't bad people. They were just immature believers who got caught up in the world's way of thinking. If we're going to find our respective places in God's plan, we must make sure we aren't so worldly that we're useless for the Kingdom.

Being a Christian in a World That Isn't

1 Corinthians 5–6

 hat's Ahead

- Seeing Sin for What It Is (5:1-8)
- Those Inside, Those Outside (5:9-13)
- Can't We All Just Get Along? (6:1-8)
- Don't Be like the Others (6:9-20)

Paul finished talking about divisions in the church by saying that a root of the problem was the spiritual pride and arrogance of the Corinthians. That thought carries over into chapters 5 and 6 of 1 Corinthians. Because of their spiritual haughtiness, the Corinthians were living in immorality, and they were actually proud of it. Paul confronts this situation head-on with a "Snap out of it!" command (only he used more biblical terminology).

Seeing Sin for What It Is (5:1-8)

The report was clear and factual: One of the Corinthian Christians was engaged in a continuing sexual affair with his stepmother. Paul was shocked—not at that type of behavior (because it was common in the city of Corinth) but at the church's acceptance of such behavior by a member of their own Christian family. Paul hammered them for being proud of their tolerance when they should have been grieving over this shameful situation.

Paul instructs the Corinthians to deal with this situation immediately. He doesn't need to be there physically, because he is with them in spirit. There are no gray areas about this circumstance. The sin is blatant, and the man's unrepentant attitude is clear. Church discipline is necessary for both the man's benefit and for the church's spiritual well-being. But Paul doesn't want a vigilante mentality. Church discipline involves an official church meeting where the sinner is confronted. If he continues to be defiant in his sin, he must be expelled from any further fellowship with the other believers.

Does this method of church discipline sound harsh? Well, it is exactly aligned with the approach Christ suggested:

> If that person [whom you have confronted with his sin] still refuses to listen, take your case to the church. If the church decides you are right, but the other person won't accept it, treat that person as a pagan or a corrupt tax collector (Matthew 18:17).

But isn't the church supposed to be loving and forgiving? Yes, and in love the church releases the unrepentant sinner to the full and natural consequences of his sin. Perhaps the downward spiral of his sin will take him to the breaking point. When he hits bottom, maybe he will turn back to God. So the church deals with the unrepentant sinner in this manner for his own good.

And the church must remove the unrepentant sinner from their fellowship for yet another reason. Sin is a virus, and if it is allowed to exist in the church unchecked, it may spread to more people. Believers need to realize that sinful behavior has consequences, and church discipline is a helpful reminder.

An Old Testament Illustration

Just as a tiny bit of yeast affects an entire lump of dough, a little sin can permeate the entire church. Paul reminds the Corinthians of the Jewish festival of Passover, which included removing leaven (the yeast) from the home and baking bread without it. At this same celebration, Jews commemorated the sacrifice of the Passover lamb. Paul reminds the Corinthians that our Passover Lamb is Jesus Christ, and He was sacrificed for our sins. The Corinthians were not bound to celebrate the Passover festival, but they should celebrate the spirit of Passover by removing the leaven of sin from their lives.

Those Inside, Those Outside (5:9-13)

A point of clarification was in order. In his earlier letter, Paul dealt with a similar situation. As with the current case, Paul told the Corinthians not to associate with the person who was ensnared in sexual immorality and refused to bring it to an end. But the Corinthians must have been a little confused about what Paul said in that earlier letter. Apparently some of them had interpreted his comments to mean that Christians should cut off contact with all non-Christians (because all unbelievers are unrepentant sinners).

"Whoa!" Paul seems to say. He makes a distinction between dealing with unbelievers and dealing with unrepentant Christians:

- He doesn't want Christians to stop associating with unbelievers. (You would have to move to another planet if that was the case.) The unsaved are doing what comes naturally for them. We, as Christians, are not supposed to judge them; that will be for God to do. We should maintain our contacts and friendships with them. We are the means by which they can see the love of Christ in action.

- But we are to take a different approach with Christians who continue in sin without repenting. Those are the people with whom we are supposed to terminate our relationships. This direction is harsh, but it is for their own benefit and our own spiritual well-being.

In but *Not* of the *World*

Some Christians make the mistake of thinking they are "spiritual" when they live in isolation from the non-Christian world. But that is contrary to what Paul tells the Corinthians. And it is not the approach that Christ had in mind for His followers. On the evening before He was crucified, Christ specifically prayed to His heavenly Father that His disciples would be able to resist temptations *of* the world while they ministered *in* the world. Here is how He said it:

> I'm not asking you to take them out of the world, but to keep them safe from the evil one (John 17:15).

> As you sent me into the world, I am sending them into the world (John 17:18).

According to John 17:20, this prayer was not only uttered for His disciples (Peter, John, and the gang), but also for "all who will ever believe in me because of their testimony" (which includes you).

Can't We All Just Get Along? (6:1-8)

Paul's discussion moves to another subject that is somewhat related to dealing with difficult people in the church. Sometimes a dispute arises between two Christians, each of whom believes he is right and the other is wrong. This was apparently a significant enough problem in the Corinthian church that the Christians were suing each other in civil court. Lawsuits were a common practice in the society, but Paul recognized this as another sign of spiritual immaturity.

Throughout the far-reaching provinces of the Roman Empire, ethnic groups had the right to settle disputes between themselves based on their own national laws (instead of the statutes of the Roman legal system). Paul urges the Corinthians to take advantage of this opportunity and to settle any civil disputes between them within the church rather than in the courts.

Paul reminds these believers that at some time in eternity future they will be assuming the role of judges.

- Here is what Jesus said about it: "I assure you that when I, the Son of Man, sit upon my glorious throne in the Kingdom, you who have been my followers will also sit on twelve thrones, judging the twelve tribes of Israel" (Matthew 19:28).

- Other passages that indicate Christians will be involved in some aspect of judging the world at the Second Coming include these: 2 Timothy 2:12; Revelation 3:21; 20:4.

- Paul also stated that Christians will judge angels. This may imply the judgment of fallen angels (see 2 Peter 2:4; Jude 1:6; Revelation 19:19-20; 20:10), or it may refer to presiding over heavenly angels during the future reign of Christ.

If Christians can handle judicial matters of eternal significance, then they should be able handle their own disputes in trivial, earthly matters.

Remember that Paul earlier elaborated on the fact the spiritual matters seem like foolishness to unbelievers. Non-Christians simply cannot understand God's paradigm. Consequently, doesn't it seem ridiculous for two Christians to submit their lawsuit to a judge who isn't going to bring a spiritual dimension to his decision?

Finally, in case his other arguments fail, Paul tries to shame the Corinthians into proper action. They prided themselves on their intellect and wisdom, so Paul asked if they didn't have at least one person in the entire church wise enough to handle such disagreements.

Pride, once again, is at the core of this problem in the Corinthian church. The self-importance of each litigant drove him to seek redress for some alleged wrong or injury he had endured. Pride was driving them to take advantage of each other. In an effort to deflate their pride, Paul tells them that being cheated would be better than taking advantage of another person.

Don't Be like the Others (6:9-20)

The Corinthians were so caught up in the culture that they were having a difficult time separating right from wrong. They were engaged in all sorts of sexual immorality (and Paul gives them a list to make sure they understand what he means). He also mentions other types of social corruptions (greed, swindling, etc.) in which they were engaged. Paul reminds them that this depraved condition was commonplace in their lives B.C. (before Christ) but that their behavior should reflect their new, right standing with God.

Apparently some of the Corinthians were living by the mantra "Since my sins have been forgiven, then I'm free to live as I please." Paul corrected their theology:

- Not everything is beneficial for a Christian.

- A Christian should refrain from those things that aren't beneficial.

A favorite saying of the day (based in Greek philosophy) went like this: "Food is for the stomach, and the stomach is for food." The Corinthians were trying to extend the logic to something like "Sexual pleasures are to be enjoyed just like food is intended to be eaten." Paul anticipates their objection and points out the fallacy in their logic:

- God intended for our bodies to eat food.

- And He intended food to be eaten.

- But God didn't intend our bodies for immorality.

- Furthermore, a Christian's body belongs to Christ.

- Therefore, as Christians we should always refrain from morally corrupt behavior.

Paul gives sound and effective advice for avoiding sexual temptations: Run away from them! (So much for the intellectual strategies of the Corinthians.) We must honor God not only with our minds but also with our bodies. We need to be forever mindful that the Holy Spirit lives in us. As Paul puts it, our bodies are "the temple of the Holy Spirit" (6:19). Our standard for living should reflect that we belong to God and He dwells within us.

Reprise: Right Thinking Leads to Right Living

The Corinthians were doing the wrong things because their thinking was twisted. Paul knew that if he could get them to think clearly, maturely, and spiritually, then their conduct would be pleasing to God.

You should be mindful of your behavior. Make sure what you do honors God. But don't overlook your thoughts. Remember that you are best able to evaluate the appropriateness of your behavior when your thinking is spiritually accurate. Correct thinking is essential preparation for service to God.

■ ■ ■

Study the Word

1. On the subject of church discipline as Paul discusses in 1 Corinthians 5:1-9, read 2 Corinthians 2:1-11 and Matthew 18:15-20. What are the principles of church discipline in these passages? If the sin of a believer is ignored, what are the risks to the individual? What are the dangers to the congregation?

2. If you got into a dispute with another Christian, how would you go about settling the disagreement? What if you can't come to some compromise? If you decided to let church members decide the outcome, would you want to impose any ground rules?

3. Why are many Christians so quick to be judgmental of the conduct of unbelievers? What would Paul say about that tendency?

4. Explain the concept of living *in* but not *of* the world. What would you say to a Christian who has no non-Christian friends?

5. Read Romans 6:15-23. Based on this passage, how would you have responded to the Corinthians' argument that they had freedom to engage in immoral behavior?

Chapter 5

Some modern liberal critics accuse
Paul of being cruel to women in this
teaching, but nothing could be further
from the truth! Paul's ministry of
the Gospel did more to raise the position
of women than people realize. Wherever
Christianity has gone, it has improved
the lot of workers, women, and children.

Warren W. Wiersbe

It Doesn't Get More Relevant than This

Critics who claim that the Bible is filled with antiquated, irrelevant myths haven't read 1 Corinthians 7. As you read this passage, you'll find that Paul is speaking directly to you, whether you are single, married, divorced, or widowed. (You've got to be in one of those categories.) He deals with those who are virgins and those who aren't. (Here again, he's got you covered.)

Paul isn't shy about the blunt realities of physical temptations. He's not oblivious to sexual urges. Don't expect to find any "Thou shalt not" references here. That's not Paul's approach. Rather, he discusses the subjects of sex, singleness, marriage, and divorce in an open and candid manner. Does that surprise you? It shouldn't. God's plan for your life is not isolated from the realities of your circumstances and personality. God knows who you are and what you need. These subjects occupy a central place in most people's lives. Consequently, God wants you to understand the dynamics of His will for your life in these important areas.

Answers About Singleness, Marriage, and Divorce

1 Corinthians 7

The Corinthians probably wouldn't have scored well on the reading comprehension portion of the SAT exam. They had completely misunderstood Paul's comments in his first letter about associating with sinful non-believers. (He straightened them out in 5:9-11.) And they also missed his points about abstaining from sexual immorality. Their twisted misinterpretations produced some strange opinions:

- All sex is sinful, so Christians shouldn't get married.

- All sex is sinful, so married Christians should be celibate.

- If a Christian is married to an unbeliever, the marriage should be dissolved.

And the list goes on. So many people in the church held some of these goofy views that the Corinthians wrote to Paul asking for some clarification. He was glad to realign their views with biblical principles.

As you read his comments, remember the context of the culture of the Corinthians. Several philosophies competed within their society:

- The Stoic view said that basic urges should be denied.

- According to the view of Epicureanism, all pleasures should be pursued.

- Some "religions" even tried to blend the other two views, advocating purging your body of immoral desires—by satisfying them.

- Women were low on the social ladder. Polygamy was common. Prostitution was openly accepted, and marriage fidelity was unheard of.

No wonder the Corinthian Christians needed some guidance.

General Principles About Marriage (7:1-9)

Don't misunderstand Paul's position. He says that an unmarried, celibate life is good, but he is not saying that singleness is a preferable lifestyle for everyone. In fact, in light of the rampant sexual temptations of the world, Paul endorses marriage between one man and one woman.

Sex plays a significant role in every marriage, so the husband and wife should understand the ground rules. Each spouse needs to respect the physical needs of the other. Sex is not a right to be demanded or a reward to be withheld. It is a gift that is to be given to the other spouse. Does this mean that a husband is entitled to expectations that exceed the interests of his wife, and that she is compelled because "the wife gives authority over her body to the husband" (7:4)? No. The directive "do not deprive each other" must be understood in the context of mutual respect for each other. (See Ephesians 5:21-33.)

Paul indicates that singleness works well for him, and Christians should consider it. Still, he doesn't downgrade marriage. He considers both circumstances to be gifts from God. But he understands the danger of temptation, so he explains that a decision to marry is better than living as a single with constant lustful thoughts.

Not Tonight. I'm Praying.

Paul gives one exception to the principle that spouses shouldn't withhold sex from each other. If they both agree, they may abstain for a period of time during which they can devote themselves to prayer. This is consistent with a tradition in the Old Testament for a time of special devotion to God that promoted prayer during periods of fasting and sexual abstinence (1 Samuel 21:4-5).

Thoughts About Divorce (7:10-16)

Paul emphasizes that his apparent earlier instructions to marry a believer should not be misinterpreted to advocate a Christian divorcing an unbelieving spouse.

Paul emphasizes that marriage should be considered permanent. Under that overarching principle, he addresses the specific situation of mixed marriages (a Christian married to a non-Christian). In such a case, the Christian should work to keep the marriage together. In other words, an unbelieving spouse is not an excuse for the Christian spouse to seek divorce. The saved spouse brings the influence of Christ into marriage. The presence of the Holy Spirit in the home is important for the children, and it may lead to the conversion of the unsaved spouse.

While permanent marriage is what God intended, Paul knows that reality doesn't always match the ideal. With loving-kindness and understanding, he adds these teachings:

- If a person leaves the marriage, he or she should remain single. Perhaps the marriage can be restored at a later time.

- If an unsaved spouse wants to terminate the marriage with a Christian spouse, then the saved spouse is not compelled to keep the marriage together.

What Does God Think of Sex?

God invented the concept of sexual intercourse, and He designed the anatomical equipment for its implementation. So He's got to be in favor of it. But He clearly intended sex for marriage only.

The Bible acknowledges that physical pleasure is one of the benefits of sex (Song of Songs 4:1-7), but it also regards sexual intercourse as a seal of the lifelong commitment made between a husband and wife. God's view of sex is more about commitment than pleasure. (Notice that the Old Testament uses marriage as an analogy of the relationship between God and Israel, and it refers to Israel's detours into idolatry as "adultery.")

Sex is best when it is used according to the Designer's specifications.

Sidebar: Stay the Way You Are (7:17-24)

Paul knows that the subject of marriage might weigh heavily on the minds of those who are single. As important as this issue is to them, Paul wants to expand their perspective as followers of Christ. He tells them to relax in their current circumstances. He doesn't want them to fret about changing the situation that God has allowed for them.

Paul uses circumcision as an example. Circumcision was a tradition for Jewish males. The first Christians were Jews, and many of them believed that circumcision should be a requirement for male Gentiles who accepted Christ. Paul spent a good portion of his missionary career saying that circumcision was fine but that it was not necessary. Neither the circumcised Christian nor the uncircumcised Christian needs to change his position to gain God's favor.

And so it is with any Christian, married or not, slave or not. One situation is not more spiritual than another. We should be content in our present situation and not stress over changing it. But note that Paul is not saying we should never change our status. We should simply seek to serve God in the circumstances He has for us in the present, and we should be content to stay there until God assigns a different situation for us.

Can We Ignore Paul's Opinions?

Paul repeats many of Christ's teachings on marriage and divorce. But sprinkled throughout 1 Corinthians 7, you'll see Paul make statements such as "This is just my opinion" or "I don't have a direct command from the Lord on this." Do such disclaimers leave us with some loopholes? Do these statements lack the authority of the rest of Scripture?

Saying that instructions are his own rather than the Lord's does not undercut the authority of what Paul says. Rather, it simply means that Jesus had said nothing on these points. Consequently, Paul had to give his opinions. If you are wondering whether his "opinions" are trustworthy and reliable, we direct you to 2 Timothy 3:16:

> *All Scripture is inspired by God and is useful to teach us what is true and to make us realize what is wrong in our lives. It straightens us out and teaches us to do what is right.*

Premarital Advice with a Spiritual Outlook (7:25-35)

Apparently the Corinthians had asked Paul's instruction for young women who were eligible for marriage. Since arranged marriages were the custom of the day, perhaps parents were asking on behalf of their daughters. Before we get to his advice, let's review the reality and the expectations that affected his response:

- *The reality:* Paul is the first to admit that marriage brings a whole set of responsibilities that will be distractions from serving God. (Marriage is ordained of God, and giving love and attention to your spouse is exactly what God wants you to do. So technically, marriage doesn't distract you from serving God, but we're sure you get Paul's point.) A single person typically has more time to devote to ministries, whereas a married person has to be using some of that time on family commitments.

- *The expectation:* The "present crisis" to which Paul refers (7:26) may be an allusion to the severe food shortage in the Mediterranean at the time. (Some scholars believe the reference is to the impending persecution that the Roman government would inflict upon Christians.) This "present crisis" did impact his response, but Paul had an even greater impending expectation: "The time that remains is very short" (7:29). Here again, scholars differ on Paul's reference. Some theologians believe Paul was talking about the imminent return of Christ. (Most first-century Christians believed that Christ would return in their lifetime.) Other scholars think this is another insinuation that Roman persecution would soon bring a halt to the Christians' ability tu openly evangelize.

Given the reality and the expectation, Paul's advice is for young people of marrying age to "remain just as you are" (7:26). If they postpone engagement and marriage, they will have greater ability to witness for Christ. Paul extends this same principle to others:

- eligible bachelors (7:32-34)

- engaged couples (7:36)

- widows who may be considering remarrying (7:39-40)

But with the same graciousness that permeates all of 1 Corinthians 7, Paul also indicates that no one in these categories would be doing wrong to marry. He is not placing restrictions upon them either way. He just wants them to take into consideration the realities of married life as they seek to follow God's will for their lives.

For Paul, the most important thing in life is to put God first. He wants his Christian brothers and sisters in Corinth to do the same thing as they consider a marriage relationship. He would want you to do the same thing.

Was Paul Married?

This is a bit of a mystery. Paul's writings comprise about one-third of the New Testament, but he never mentions a wife. The biographical sketches of him in Acts don't suggest that he is married. So, no wife, right?

But wait. Before Paul became a Christian, he was a member of the Sanhedrin (the chief judicial counsel of the Jews). Members of the Sanhedrin had to be married. So, he must have had a wife, right?

But wait. You might remember Paul saying, "It is better to stay unmarried, just as I am" (7:8). So what was it? Wife or no wife?

Most scholars believe that Paul was married (while a member of the Sanhedrin), but his wife died at some unknown time. When he wrote 1 Corinthians, he was probably a widower. Thus he speaks from experience on the subjects of both singleness and marriage.

■ ■ ■

$\mathcal{S}$tudy the $\mathcal{W}$ord

1. Why might Paul have placed this discourse about marriage immediately after his discussion about avoiding sexual sin (6:9-20)?

2. What additional insights about sex and marriage can you gain from Proverbs 5; Proverbs 7; and Song of Songs 4:1-7?

3. Read Matthew 19:1-12. What does this passage teach about divorce?

4. Read through 1 Corinthians 7:17-24. Look for the repeated references to God "calling" us to salvation or to service. What point is Paul trying to emphasize?

5. Other than marriage, what are some "realities" of life that you should consider as possible distractions from your service to Christ?

Chapter 6

The primary purpose of Paul's not taking full advantage of his Christian liberty was that he might win the more.... [He] was willing to do anything and to sacrifice anything to win people to Jesus Christ. As far as his rights were concerned he was free from all men, but because of his love for all men he would gladly limit those rights for their sakes. He had, figuratively, become a slave to all. He would modify his habits, his preferences, and his entire lifestyle if any of those things caused someone to stumble, to be offended, or to be hindered from faith in the Lord.

John MacArthur

What's That Again?

With all the talk of sexual immorality and marriage, you might have lost sight of the fact that 1 and 2 Corinthians can help you find your unique place in God's plan. By now, you know enough to realize that Paul isn't going to tell you the precise specifics of God's will for your life. But he has provided you with some foundational truths for ascertaining your role in God's design.

- Reject the world's mind-set because it is contrary to God's spiritual paradigm (1:25).

- You've got to start thinking correctly (biblically) in order to start living spiritually (3:18).

- You shouldn't isolate yourself from unbelievers just because they are sinners, but you must avoid associating with Christians who are arrogantly unrepentant (5:9-11).

- Even in big decisions such as getting married, the important thing is to put God first (7:35).

Paul isn't finished with his primer on preparing to know and do God's will. He's got several other essential principles, and the one in this chapter might catch you by surprise. It's all about refraining from doing something that is totally permissible to do.

If you want to know God's will and your place in it, this chapter is required reading because you're not likely to figure this one out on your own.

Love Limits Liberty

1 Corinthians 8–10

*B*eginning with 1 Corinthians 7, Paul responds directly to questions raised in a letter from those confused Christians in Corinth. You can tell that Paul is working his way down a checklist:

- "Now about the questions you asked in your letter" (7:1)

- "Now let's talk about food that has been sacrificed to idols" (8:1)

- "And now, dear brothers and sisters, I will write about the special abilities the Holy Spirit gives to each of us" (12:1)

- "Now about the money being collected for the Christians in Jerusalem" (16:1)

You read that second one correctly: The Corinthians asked about the propriety of eating meat offered to idols. At this point you might be tempted to skip a few pages in your Bible reading because you don't see the relevance of this discussion to your twenty-first-century life. (After all, your dietary consumption habits probably don't include idol-offered meat.) Don't be too quick to dismiss the relevance of Paul's message. First Corinthians 8–10 teaches us how to govern our conduct according to our consideration for other believers.

*W*here in *C*orinth *C*an *Y*ou *G*et a *G*ood *J*uicy *S*teak?

If you were a beef lover in Corinth, you wouldn't go to a fancy restaurant or a butcher shop to satisfy your red meat cravings. You'd go straight to the pagan temple. Here's why:

- Romans and Greeks were polytheistic (they worshipped many gods).

- They also believed that evil spirits attempted to invade humans by penetrating certain foods before they were consumed.

- They regularly sacrificed their best livestock before the idols of their gods. This achieved the dual purposes of worship and cleansing the meat of any parasitic demons.

- Some of the idol-offered meat was burned on the altar, some was given to the pagan priests (as compensation for services), and some was returned to the worshipper. Those priests ended up with much more meat than they could eat, so they sold the excess in their temple butcher shop.

- The meat that a worshipper retained or that was purchased at the temple was the finest available. It was quality meat to begin with, and it had the additional benefit of a "temple cleansed" stamp of approval. If you were having company over for dinner, your guests deserved nothing less than the temple's best.

What's the Beef over Idols' Meat? (8:1-13)

Remember that Paul was dealing with immature Christians who prided themselves in their knowledge of all things. Paul begins his discourse by telling them that they don't know as much as they think they know. And in the church, knowledge isn't nearly as useful as love.

The Corinthians do have some important facts straight:

- The one and only true God is found in Jesus Christ.

- No other gods exist, and idols are nothing more than shelf ornaments.

But Paul points out that many new converts to Christianity may not have this knowledge. Most of them came out of polytheistic beliefs, so they might acknowledge Christ as God but still believe that lesser gods exist. For these less knowledgeable Christians, eating meat that has been offered to idols bothers their conscience; they connect it to the worship of real gods. Their view is wrong, but it is something they sincerely believe.

Even though nothing is wrong with eating such meat, the more knowledgeable Christians should refrain from doing so if the immature converts think that it is sin. In other words, mature believers should restrict their behavior out of consideration for the less mature Christian. To do otherwise might cause the immature Christian to "stumble" into sin.

A Stumbling Block

Think of a young boy who admires an older brother. That older brother has to watch his conduct around the younger sibling. While certain things are permissible for the older brother, the younger child may not be mature enough to handle them. And the youngster may not appreciate important distinctions or circumstances. If the older brother is doing something that is proper for his age but that the younger brother considers to be wrong, then that younger child may become confused about the importance of doing what is right. (This is the old "hey, if he can do it, why can't I?" mentality.) In this case, the older brother has caused the younger brother to "stumble."

Letting Go of Liberties (9:1-27)

Paul has just explained that Christians should voluntarily limit their freedoms in situations that might adversely impact another Christian. If something might impede someone else's spiritual growth, then the mature Christian should gladly refrain from doing it—even if it is otherwise entirely appropriate to do.

To illustrate this principle further, this time without meat, Paul uses a personal example. He has refused to receive compensation from the Corinthians. Here is how he lays out his argument:

1. *His apostleship:* Paul makes the case for being an apostle. The Christian community respected the authority of apostles because they were the leaders of the early Christian faith. (Even if some people are suspect of his apostolic credentials, Paul says that

the Corinthians have personal knowledge of his ministry, so they shouldn't discount his status as an apostle.)

2. *His entitlement:* Paul was basically an itinerant missionary. Because he traveled to establish churches and teach in them, he didn't have a regular job. Churches often provided food, clothing, housing, and some remuneration for such missionaries.

3. *Common sense:* Paul gives several illustrations of workers who receive benefits that naturally flow from their labor. A soldier doesn't have to pay his own expenses. The oxen eat the grain as they pull the threshing wheel. The shepherd is allowed to drink the goats' milk from the herd he cares for. The farmhand gets a share of the grain. (Note: This line of reasoning does not justify your stealing office supplies or a fax machine from your cubicle at work. You are getting a paycheck; the farmhand didn't.)

4. *His rationale for declining payment:* Paul didn't want the issue of money to interfere with his ministry. He didn't want anyone to think that he was preaching out of any other motivation than to spread the Good News. Because any compensation he might receive could possibly be an obstacle, he wanted to remove the issue by refusing any financial assistance.

Being an effective Christian requires vigilant sensitivity. You've got to be aware of who you are with and what you are doing. Acceptable behavior with one group might be inappropriate in another group. Does this mean that a Christian is inherently hypocritical (or schizophrenic)? Not at all. Remember that we are talking about behavior that is entirely permissible for the mature Christian. But freedom to engage in such activities may need to be tempered by restraint when other people are involved. In Paul's case, he had to adapt his conduct according to his associations with unsaved Jews, unsaved Greeks, or Christians. (That covered the gamut. In the circles Paul traveled, everybody fit into one of those three groups.) He was willing to forfeit his freedoms so that he could find common ground where he could share his faith.

An Athletic Analogy

Paul concludes chapter 9 with an allusion to athletic games (which would be very familiar to any self-respecting resident of ancient Greece). Paul mentions the self-discipline of an athlete. The athlete forsakes certain privileges and freedoms because he doesn't want to do anything that might hurt his training regimen and jeopardize his victory.

Like an athlete, Paul wants to stay in strict training, staying away from anything that impedes progress toward his goal of winning the eternal prize.

Paul makes an interesting comment about being "disqualified." He is not intending to suggest that he worries about losing his salvation. That is not a possibility for Paul or any other Christian. Rather, he doesn't want to be disqualified from receiving rewards at the Judgment Seat of Christ (see the earlier discussion on pages 40–41.)

All to the Glory of God (10:1-33)

Paul isn't ready to leave the "meat offered to idols" issue. He wants to repeat his lesson about prioritizing love for others over Christian liberty, and he wants to raise a danger about eating temple meat that the "knowledgeable" Corinthian Christians hadn't considered.

- *The hidden danger:* Paul doesn't want these Corinthians, caught up in the pride of their knowledge, to think that they can hang out in the pagan temples to buy meat without running spiritual risks. The immorality and pagan rituals did not create a spiritually healthy environment. Placing yourself in evil surroundings puts you at risk of succumbing to temptation. Paul proves this warning by pointing to the history of the Israelites. Despite the spiritual blessings that God had bestowed upon them, they continually turned to the immoral ways and the idol worship of the neighboring pagan cultures. (Furthermore, as Christians we shouldn't be in such places. We belong to the body of Christ. That is the principle we celebrate at communion—the Lord's Supper—when believers all eat from the same loaf of bread. Because of our spiritual connection to Christ and each other, we shouldn't expose ourselves to evil influences. We ought to stay firmly connected with the former and completely cut off from the latter.)

- *The lesson repeated:* The issue is not about meat. The real question is how Christians choose to use their freedom. They should not exercise it selfishly. They should temper it with love for less mature believers.

Paul suggests a better test for such controversies. Is it right or wrong? is not the right question. The more pertinent inquiry is this: Is this behavior likely to interfere with someone else's spiritual growth? If so, then we should enthusiastically refrain from exercising our freedom because our sole purpose should be to glorify God and direct others to Him. Paul succinctly summarizes this entire discourse:

*Whatever you eat or drink or whatever you do,
you must do all for the glory of God* (10:31).

One More Verse

Paul didn't divide his letter into chapters and verses. (That was done centuries later by scribes.) Most scholars include the first verse of 1 Corinthians 11 with Paul's previous discussion. After all, he has just said that he doesn't do what is best for him, but rather does what is best for others so they might be saved (10:33). That is exactly the attitude that he wants the Corinthians to have. Thus, it makes sense that he would conclude by saying, "And you should follow my example, just as I follow Christ's" (11:1).

■ ■ ■

Study the Word

1. The three chapters of 1 Corinthians 8–10 are focused on a single theme. In your own words, describe the point Paul emphasizes.

2. The notion of forfeiting your rights goes against the prevailing mind-set in our society. Do you agree with Paul's premise? Explain your answer.

3. What is a contemporary equivalent to the "meat offered to idols" controversy? What do you have Christian freedom to do that less mature Christians may consider inappropriate?

4. Do you agree with Paul that spiritual dangers are associated with placing yourself in immoral surroundings (even though you may be doing nothing wrong)? Can you think of some examples?

5. Might a weak believer be so immature that his or her stance should no longer limit your liberty?

Chapter 7

The theme of personal freedom exercised
without regard for the need of others or
the glory of God [from the previous passages
of 1 Corinthians] seems no less a part
of this section which deals with practices
affecting the assembly of the church. Here
too Paul responded to the Corinthians'
spirit of self-indulgence by stressing
the principle of glorifying God and
building up each other in the church.

David K. Lowery

It's Not About You

In the course of our travels, we meet many people who express a sincere desire to discover God's will for their life. We probably haven't met you yet, but we expect that you're on a similar quest to find out just exactly what God wants you to do.

Sometimes people state their intentions this way: "I want to do great things for God." We know what they mean, but we cringe a little bit when we hear people say that. Christians must be careful that their motivations are pure. Our intent should be to do things for our God, who is great, not to do things for Him that will make us look great.

This is more than a matter of semantics. It is a real problem for many Christians. It was for the Corinthian Christians. As you are about to read, they were guilty of behavior during worship ceremonies that was self-centered. At a time when the focus should have been on Christ, they were worried about themselves.

Let your study of this passage be "gut check" time. What are your motivations for serving the Lord? Are you anxious to serve Him because you might get a little recognition along the way? Are you only willing to do great things for God? Or are you willing to do anything for God, who is great?

Worshipping God the Way He Deserves

1 Corinthians 11

*D*on't be caught off guard. The Scripture passages you'll be reading in this chapter appear at first glance to be mired in first-century customs and traditions. Most likely, in your personal cultural experience, no one is insisting on women wearing veils in public, short hair on a woman is not a disgrace, and long hair on a man is not an abomination (although it may be an outdated throwback to the 1970s). But don't regard Paul's comments as irrelevant to you simply because they refer to ancient Mediterranean cultural practices. Look at the reasoning and spiritual principles on which he bases his comments. Biblical truth doesn't change, so these concepts are very much relevant to your contemporary life (regardless of your hairstyle).

Get Your Head into Worship (11:1-16)

A few contemporary scholars have misinterpreted Paul's teachings and considered him to be sexist. But that was probably not the opinion of women in the first century. They undoubtedly appreciated Paul's outspoken (and radical) teaching that women had equal dignity with men. (Remember 7:3-4?) The women in Corinth wanted to celebrate (and perhaps flaunt) their equal worth and value. Paul compliments them for following his teaching, but he needs to correct the manner in which they are expressing this equality.

Here's the problem in a nutshell: The Christian women in Corinth thought that their equality with men meant that they should *act* like men. They were rejecting the traditional apparel of women (a veil in worship services) and dressing like men (with their heads uncovered). Paul doesn't want them to be ashamed of being women or to adopt the behavior of men. Rather, they should find their value and significance in being the godly women that God intends for them to be.

We can better understand the "veil" issue with some cultural background. Historian Sir William Anderson has written this:

> In Oriental lands, the veil is the power and the honor and the dignity of the woman.... But without the veil the woman is a thing of ought, whom any man may insult.... A woman's authority and dignity vanish along with the all-covering veil that she discards.

Paul was telling the Corinthian Christians—both the men and the women—that they should behave in ways that are honorable in their culture. Because the culture of the time shamed women who entered worship without a veil, women should keep their heads covered. Similarly, because short hair on a woman was a sign of being a prostitute and long hair on a male meant the same thing, Paul instructs the church to follow the customs that will not damage their reputation for Christ. Certainly Paul is not advocating following all of society's trends and fads, but he encourages conformity with behavior that will enhance our message as ambassadors for Christ. (Remember that in 10:29-33 he had talked about not being offensive to anyone so that everything could be done to the glory of God.)

Are You Having a Hardship with Headship?

Paul's use of the "headship" principle in 11:3 has prompted confusion and controversy. The problem is that "head" doesn't usually mean to us what it meant to the Corinthians. When someone refers to a person as the "head" of a company, we understand that to mean that the person is in charge and every other employee is subordinate. But that's not the meaning Paul intends when he says that "the head of every man is Christ, and the head of the woman is man" (11:3 NIV).

Paul is talking about the *origin* or the *source* of our existence. Thus, Christ is the head of man because Christ is the source of all life (Ephesians 1:22; Colossians 1:16-18). Because Eve was created from the rib of Adam (Genesis 2:21-22), so man is the origin of woman.

Paul's context also includes a sense of responsibility. Christ is the "head" of the church in that He holds it together (Ephesians 4:15-16). In a similar way, the husband is the "head" of the family and provides protection and spiritual leadership for his wife and children. (See Ephesians 6:4.)

Paul's use of "headship" has to do with a chain of responsibility and not different brackets of value of individuals.

Think of It This Way

Our society functions best with an orderly arrangement of social responsibilities even though all individuals have the same worth. So for example, a police officer has responsibility for law enforcement, but that doesn't mean he is a better person than you (even though he can cite you for speeding). And law enforcement officers may be responsible to sacrifice their life for your safety (although you are not obligated to risk injury for their protection).

Paul uses the "headship" of Christ for humanity and of husbands for wives in a similar sense. It has everything to do with a chain of responsibility and nothing to do with differing levels of significance or value. Its aspect of selfless love—Christ's for the church (Ephesians 5:29) and husbands' for wives (Ephesians 5:25)—is something to be appreciated rather than despised.

Terrible Table Manners (11:17-22)

Some call it "communion." Others call it "the Lord's Supper." It is the commemoration of the Passover meal that Christ shared with His disciples on the evening before His crucifixion. At that meal, Christ announced a new covenant. (Under God's prior covenant with Israel, God forgave sins when a priest sacrificed an animal on an altar. Under the "new covenant," a person can have a direct relationship with God because Christ was the "sacrificial Lamb" whose death was sufficient to cover the penalty for sins.) Christ gave symbolism to the new covenant with the eating of bread and drinking of wine. He said that the bread was representative of His body; the wine was representative of the blood that He would shed on the cross. Although the disciples didn't understand the significance of what He was saying at the time, He told them that in the future they should use the bread and wine to remember His death.

And so the Corinthian Christians regularly celebrated the Lord's Supper. But in predictable Corinthian style, they were behaving in a way that brought improper attention to themselves and diverted the worship of Christ:

- The custom was to celebrate the Lord's Supper when eating a dinner together as a church family. In what must have been the precursor to church potluck dinners, each person in the Corinthian church brought his or her own food for the dinner. This resulted in the rich Christians having an excessive feast, while poor Christians had meager portions. The disparity between the well-fed upper class and the starving lower class was a source of friction in the church, and it was disgraceful in God's sight.

- Some of the wealthy were turning this solemn ceremony into a party. They showed no restraint or decorum and were getting drunk. Paul couldn't believe such behavior could occur at the communion ceremony, not even in Corinth.

The Corinthians weren't fooling Paul. He knew that their Lord's Supper celebrations had nothing to do with Christ for many of them. It was an excuse to have a raucous time without making a mess in their own homes.

Putting Christ Back into Communion (11:23-34)

By retelling the story of the original celebration of the Lord's Supper, Paul reminds the Corinthians that the focus of the event should be entirely on Christ. No one should do anything to degrade the observance.

This was not some meaningless ritual that the Corinthians were participating in. Perhaps it was to some of the Corinthians, but not to Paul. And certainly not to Christ. Paul lets them know that God takes this ceremony very seriously because it commemorates the crucifixion of His Son. Paul goes so far as to speculate that some people in the Corinthian church might have experienced God's discipline (in sickness or even death) because of their totally irreverent and crudely sacrilegious behavior.

*W*hat's the *R*elevance to *Y*ou?

We don't know what church you attend, but we guess that you are not gorging yourself at the communion ceremony. (In fact, stuffing yourself would be impossible at most churches that celebrate the Lord's Supper with a thimble-size cup of grape juice and a cracker crumb.) So what is the relevance of this passage to you?

Don't overlook the specific guidelines that Paul gave to the Corinthians about their attitude during communion. These same guidelines apply to you:

- You should thoughtfully reflect on the fact that Christ died for you (11:26).

- You should participate respectfully to avoid dishonoring this sacred ceremony (11:27).

- You should use the occasion as an opportunity for self-examination to see if you have any unconfessed sin in your life (11:28).

- You should appreciate the company of your fellow believers and recognize that Christ's work on the cross makes you all part of one family (11:33-34).

Always one to be practical about spiritual matters (and also being one with a twinge of sarcastic humor), Paul has a suggestion for those who have been abusing the celebration of communion: If you are hungry, eat at home before you come to the Lord's Supper! Actually, that's good advice for all of us. Not the preemptive meal suggestion, but the thought that we should prepare ourselves in advance. Take heed of Paul's suggestion and spend time in prayer and in the Word immediately prior to the next time your church observes the Lord's Supper. You're likely to find that Christ is more prominent in communion than He has ever been before to you.

This Is My Body

Theologians disagree about the meaning behind Christ's statement when He took the bread and said, "This is my body" (Luke 22:19). They offer three viewpoints. Some Catholic scholars say the bread and wine actually become Christ's body and blood as they are taken at communion. Others, such as Lutherans, say that the composition of the bread and wine remains the same, but Christ is spiritually present in them. According to what may be the more widely held position, the bread and wine are merely symbolic reminders of Christ's body and blood. Regardless of these different views, one thing remains true: Christ is present with believers at the celebration of the Lord's Supper, and He deserves our full attention and devotion at that time.

■ ■ ■

Study the Word

1. What is Paul's concept of "headship" in the context of husbands and wives?

2. What personal applications can you draw from 1 Corinthians 11:1-16?

3. Have your impressions of communion deepened during this study? If so, how?

4. What are some of the ways in which you might have been disrespectful about communion in the past?

5. What could your church do to make the celebration of communion more meaningful? What can you do to make the Lord's Supper more spiritually significant to you?

Chapter 8

Many people in Paul's day were making much of the spiritual gifts which Paul mentions. They were coveting the more showy gifts, such as speaking with tongues. The Corinthian Christians were using these gifts as ends in themselves. Many people today, like the Corinthians of old, pray constantly for the power of the Spirit. They forget that all the gifts which God gives were given that Christ might be exalted and others blessed. If God gives me any little gift at all, He gives it not that I may gather people about myself, but that it may, through me, be a blessing for others.

Henrietta C. Mears

ℛead with 𝒞aution

The three chapters of Scripture covered in this part of our study may prove to be very interesting to you. Whether you know it or not, God has empowered you by the Holy Spirit in a unique way for ministry. The special "spiritual gifts" that God has given you will allow you to serve Christ with supernatural abilities. Don't you think your spiritual gifts might be connected to the place God has for you in His plan? Learning about your spiritual gifts will give you some clear guidance about what God has in store for you.

But don't make the mistake of the Corinthians. They were so focused on their spiritual gifts that they forgot an even more important aspect of their faith. If you make a similar mistake, you'll likely get off track and miss the strategy of God's design for your life. For this reason, you must read carefully (although the title to this chapter will give you a huge clue).

Wrap Your Spiritual Gifts in Love

1 Corinthians 12–14

What you've read so far in 1 Corinthians dealt with the problems of carnality. Now we are at a turning point at which Paul will talk about spiritual practicalities. As he is dictating this letter, he is probably glad to shake off the burdens of what he has previously said, breathe a sigh of relief, and then move to a more positive subject: "And now, dear brothers and sisters, I will write more about the special abilities the Holy Spirit gives to each of us" (12:1). But everything he has to say isn't positive. In fact, Paul begins his discourse on spiritual gifts by correcting the Corinthians' skewed view of spiritual gifts.

Now About Spiritual Gifts (12:1-11)

Pagan rituals in the first century included trances, seizures, rantings, and ecstatic utterances. People perceived such behavior as the presence of a god within the individual. Physical conduct of this sort presented quite a spectacle. Coming from a background such as this, the Corinthian Christians were enamored with spiritual gifts that had an element of the spectacular; they were not as interested in spiritual gifts that were less flamboyant. Furthermore, they were inclined to give credibility to anyone who engaged in such ecstatic behavior even though people were sometimes chanting curses against God.

At the beginning of a three-chapter discourse on spiritual gifts, Paul tells the Corinthians what should have been obvious to them: Someone who is cursing Jesus is not controlled by the Holy Spirit and acting under the supernatural influence of God. (In other words, a lot of fakes are out there.) He doesn't need to belabor the point because it is so obvious.

---

*W*ould a *D*efinition *B*e *H*elpful?

A spiritual gift is a God-given, supernatural ability to serve others in a special way. It may take the form of a special power of performance, or maybe knowledge, or sensitivity.

Don't confuse a spiritual gift with a natural talent or ability. Those are gifts from God too, but not the kind Paul is referring to. Your natural abilities and talents are matters of your genetics; a spiritual gift is unrelated to the gene pool you're swimming in.

Next, Paul attempts to have the Corinthians consider the benefits of all gifts rather than focusing on utterances alone (known as "speaking in tongues" in the spiritual gifts glossary). His angle is to lay out the basic truths about spiritual gifts:

- Just as the ways we serve in the church and the ways that God works in our lives are varied, spiritual gifts are varied (12:4).

- The Holy Spirit is the source of all spiritual gifts (12:4,11).

- Every believer has at least one spiritual gift (12:7).

- The purpose of all spiritual gifts is to benefit the entire church (12:7).

- Spiritual gifts shouldn't be a subject of jealousy or rivalry because the Holy Spirit is responsible for deciding who gets which spiritual gifts (12:11).

Because the Corinthians were interested primarily in the gift of tongues, Paul gives a list of some of the other spiritual gifts. In this passage he doesn't give a definition for each gift, but we will give you a clue:

- *Wisdom* (12:8)—A Holy Spirit–inspired revelation of a solution to an immediate problem.

- *Knowledge* (12:8)—The supernatural ability to know some fact that would be impossible to know except from divine relation.

- *Faith* (12:9)—The God-given ability to believe God for the supply of a very specific need.

- *Healing* (12:9)—A supernatural power to heal someone's illness or physical defect.

- *Miracles* (12:10)—A divine power to perform supernatural acts.

- *Prophecy* (12:10)—An ability from the Holy Spirit to know and speak a specific message that God wants delivered to His people.

- *Discernment* (12:10)—An extraordinary ability to discern truth and know whether a decision or comment is aligned with God's will.

- *Tongues* (12:10)—The supernatural capability to speak in a language that the person who is speaking it does not know.

- *Interpretation of tongues* (12:10)—The Holy Spirit's power to interpret a message spoken in tongues so that the group can understand what is being said.

Body Parts (12:12-31)

The point of this passage is simple and straightforward: Our spiritual gifts may differ, but we are all essential parts of Christ's body (the church). The church won't function properly if any of our gifts are missing, so we ought to appreciate each person's giftedness and work together. (See 12:27.)

Paul makes his point by analogizing the church (and all its members) to a human body (and all its parts). Just like the parts of the human body, the members of the church are interconnected and interdependent. The human body only survives as each part functions according to its purpose; similarly, the church operates best when each person's gifts are put to use. Some parts of the body get more attention (like the eyes), while others are often forgotten (like the pancreas). Similarly, some roles in the church are higher profile, while others go unnoticed—yet all are essential.

In discussing the various "parts of the body" and the different roles and ministries of the church they perform, Paul mentions a few more spiritual gifts (in 12:28) that he doesn't include in his earlier list:

- *Apostleship*—A God-given ability to establish churches (such as Paul and the other disciples did when they brought the Gospel to regions of the world that had not yet been exposed to Christianity).

- *Teaching*—A supernatural skill for explaining the truth of God's Word in a way that is correct as well as relevant and practical.

- *Serving*—A divine awareness of needs within the Christian community, and the power to get the job done.

- *Administration*—A Holy Spirit-directed use of judgment and people skills for leadership within the church.

What Love Has Got to Do with It (13:1-13)

Imagine the surprise of the Corinthians—all hyped up about those externally expressive gifts—when they read in 12:31 that Paul is about to tell them something that is better than any of the spiritual gifts. Then he drops the bombshell: Love is more important than spiritual gifts. Do you suppose the Corinthians felt let down when Paul told them that their gifts (such as tongues, prophecy, faith, or helps), are all meaningless without love (13:1-3)?

Apparently, the meaning of Christian love was a bit fuzzy to the Corinthians. Lest they consider it to be just some philosophical notion, Paul gives some concrete definitions to the term. In 13:4-7, Paul lists approximately

15 qualities of love. This is the famous "love passage" that is often read at weddings, and certainly these characteristics should be present in every marriage. But Paul had a broader scope in mind. These are not just traits for the husband-wife relationship. Every Christian should be exhibiting all of these characteristics, all of the time, in every relationship. After all, Christ is love, and we should reflect His nature (1 John 4:7-8).

Paul also emphasizes the permanence of love. After this present life, spiritual gifts will come to an end. But love will remain. Paul wants the Corinthians to consider spiritual gifts with a long-term perspective. They should not get caught up in spiritual gift euphoria to the neglect of the more eternal qualities of faith, hope, and love. Especially love.

*W*hy the *L*ove *L*ecture?

The Corinthians thought that someone's spirituality was determined by his or her prominence, success, or expressive gifts. Paul wants them to know that this is the wrong criterion for assessing spirituality in their leaders. Instead, the test should be whether evidence of love is present in the person's relationships.

Tongues Aren't for Others (14:1-25)

Love is directed outward; it is not self-centered. So Paul logically applies that perspective to the use of spiritual gifts within the church. For this reason, he encourages the Corinthians to desire gifts that will build up the entire church rather than to focus on tongues, which doesn't benefit others.

Paul makes his point by contrasting the gift of prophecy with the gift of tongues:

- Tongues is a conversation with God, not with other people.
- Tongues is in a language no one else understands, so they get no benefit from hearing it.
- Tongues only strengthens the person who is speaking.

In sharp contrast, the gift of prophecy strengthens the entire church. These words of God, which are spoken for all to understand, give encouragement and guidance.

And what about unbelievers who may attend a worship service? Sure, the gift of tongues may convince a non-Christian that a supernatural dimension is present, but those utterances won't tell them anything about Christ. (And don't forget that pagan rituals were filled with ecstatic mutterings as well.) Paul says that unbelievers in a church meeting are going to be confronted with the Gospel message as they hear words of prophecy and the preaching of the Word.

Paul isn't saying that prophecy is the best spiritual gift, and he isn't saying that tongues is a worthless one. He is just trying to make a point to guide the Corinthians in their understanding and priorities:

> Since you are so eager to have spiritual gifts, ask God for those that will be of real help to the whole church (14:12).

Let's Have Order in the Church (14:26-40)

Church services in Corinth must have been pretty rowdy with the drunks at communion and everyone trying to outdo the others in a display of flamboyant spiritual gifts. To restore dignity and reverence to the Corinthians' services, Paul gives them some guidelines for worship. Anticipating that he might get a little resistance on these points, he boldly states that anyone claiming to have knowledge or a word from God on these points will certainly agree with what he is saying.

In light of Paul's emphasis on not bringing attention to yourself in the use of your spiritual gifts, and using gifts in a manner that benefits others more than yourself, Paul's instructions for worship make sense:

- No more than two or three should speak in tongues.

- They should speak one at a time.

- No one should speak in tongues unless someone concurrently exercises the gift of interpretation of tongues so that the others benefit from the message.

Similar principles apply in the public use of the gift of prophecy.

The bottom line is this: Our God is not a God of chaos. He is a God of order. The Holy Spirit, acting through the spiritual gifts in Christians, will not be interrupting Himself nor disrupting sincere worship of Christ Jesus. In fact, these are danger signs that the Holy Spirit is not involved with what is going on.

*A*nd *N*ow a *W*ord to the *L*adies

This is where Paul gets a bad rap for being against women. In two verses (14:34-35), Paul suggests a restriction on female input during the service. (That's a nice way of paraphrasing the verse: "Women should be silent during the church meetings" [14:34].) Does this mean that women should be gagged during church and relegated to menial, nonverbal ministries like passing out cookies and working in the nursery (provided they don't actually talk to the babies)? Absolutely not. Earlier in 1 Corinthians Paul stated that the value of women was equal to that of men.

So what's the meaning of his restriction?

- Some scholars see this as a carryover from Jewish tradition. (Women were not permitted to speak at Jewish synagogues.) But this interpretation seems weak in light of Paul's earlier discussion that Jewish traditions didn't have to be followed by Gentile Christians.

- Other theologians believe it was consistent with the cultural standards of the time. If speaking openly in a public meeting was "improper" for a woman, then Paul doesn't want Christian women doing so in church. This position is consistent with Paul's view that Christians should relinquish certain freedoms to avoid offending others and interfering with their finding Christ (10:32).

- A third interpretation is more contextual and views 14:34-35 as part of the discussion about evaluating prophecy that is spoken during the church service (14:29-33). Maybe Paul means that women are not to be the ones who "evaluate" the validity of the prophecy (14:29), although they need not be silent in other circumstances (see 11:5). This position is consistent with Paul's earlier "chain of authority" discussion (11:3-4) and his teaching in 1 Timothy 2:11-15 which delegates authoritative teaching to the role of male elders.

◼ ◼ ◼

Study the Word

1.   What characteristics are common to all spiritual gifts?

2. Paul ends chapter 12 with an interesting comment. He says that the Corinthians "should desire the most helpful gifts." Review the list of spiritual gifts that Paul mentions. Which ones is he referring to? Which ones don't qualify to be in this category? Why do you think he said this to the Corinthians?

3. How would you define "love" as that term is used most often in our culture? Contrast that with Paul's definition.

4. What standards have you used to determine whether someone is spiritual and a worthy Christian role model? According to 1 Corinthians 13, what criteria should you be using?

5. Have you identified your spiritual gifts? Which do you think you have? Describe a situation in which you've been able to use them. If you aren't sure of your spiritual gifts, which ones do you desire to have?

Chapter 9

We have come to a chapter that can be classified as one of the most important and crucial chapters of the Bible. If you would select ten of the greatest chapters of the Bible—which men have done from the beginning of the Christian era—you will find that 1 Corinthians 15 will be on your list and has been on practically all the lists ever made. It is that important. It is so important that it actually answers the first heresy of the church, which was the denial of the bodily resurrection of the Lord Jesus Christ.

J. Vernon McGee

If You Were
to *Invent a Religion...*

We don't want you to abandon your Christianity, so we are speaking hypothetically. Suppose you wanted to invent your own religion. If you want people to believe your doctrine, you better base your belief on "facts" that can't be disproved. Stay away from making up places and dates (because those can be investigated). And whatever you do, don't make up any "fact" that people could contradict with verifiable evidence.

As you are about to read, Paul violates these rules. (Of course, he wasn't dealing with a fictional god.) He points to an event—the resurrection—and says that our faith is worthless if it didn't happen. He hangs everything on that one occurrence.

The resurrection is important because it proves our faith. But more than that, it gives hope and direction for our living. As we will be discussing, knowing God's will for your life is important not only for what you are presently doing but also for where you are going. The doctrine of the resurrection explains the goal you are working toward.

The Resurrection:
There's No Denying It
1 Corinthians 15–16

What's Ahead

- Christ Really Rose from the Dead...(15:1-11)
- ...And So Will You (15:12-34)
- A New and Improved Resurrection Body (15:35-58)
- Final Instructions and Tentative Plans (16:1-24)

*U*p until now, Paul has been dealing primarily with the behavior of the Corinthians (or more properly, their misbehavior). Now his letter shifts to a doctrinal mode in which he talks less about what they *do* and more about what they *believe*.

At issue is the bodily resurrection of Christ from the grave. This concept was totally foreign to the prevailing Greek and Roman philosophies. They scoffed at Christians for believing such a notion. The Corinthian Christians were overly sensitive about the secular society's assessment of their intelligence. They were apparently standing strong in their belief of Christ's resurrection. However, they were faltering in their assurance of their own future resurrection.

Christ Really Rose from the Dead...(15:1-11)

Have you ever looked for a good definition of the Gospel (or the Good News) of Christianity? Well, Paul gives you a complete yet succinct definition in 15:3-4. Notice the significance of each element of his definition:

- *Christ died for our sins...*

  Christ was crucified. That historical fact is not in doubt. But Christianity is premised on the fact that Christ's death paid the penalty for our sins. (See Romans 3:23-25.)

- *...just as the Scriptures said.*

  This is a reference to the Old Testament Scriptures. Christ's death was not an accident. God planned and predicted it centuries before it happened. Sometimes the Old Testament references are foreshadowing allusions (such as Abraham offering to sacrifice his son Isaac); other times the references are prophetic descriptions (such as Isaiah 53).

- *He was buried...*

  Don't overlook the significance of this fact. It proves that He didn't vanish and that His body didn't disappear. His body was placed in the grave. And those who handled Christ's body after His death knew Him. They didn't mistakenly put some other corpse in the tomb. The physical body of Christ was entombed.

- *...and he was raised from the dead on the third day...*

  The empty tomb is proof of it all. Proof that Jesus is God. Proof that He has power over death. Proof that He was capable of paying the penalty for our sin because He is not otherwise guilty of sin Himself.

- *...as the Scriptures said.*

   Christianity is not a fictitious religion based on some spin doctor's interpretation of events. Rather, Christianity is proved by events that occurred precisely as the prophets of God predicted them centuries earlier. God has always had a plan, and the events of Christ's life prove that human history is moving in accordance with God's plan (which ought to give you comfort as you contemplate following God's specific plan for your life).

The resurrection of Christ didn't happen in secret. It was not a clandestine event that only one or two individuals witnessed. It was a public spectacle. Hundreds of people were witness to it. Paul lists some of the groups of people who saw Christ in His resurrected body. Paul makes the list himself, although he is included at the end. He wasn't present when the resurrected Christ was on earth, but the resurrected Christ confronted Paul years later in Paul's famous Damascus Road conversion experience. (See Acts 9:3-6.)

What Did Secular Historians Say About the Resurrection?

Critics and skeptics of the Christian faith say that the eyewitness accounts of the resurrection by the disciples and other followers of Christ aren't credible. (Apparently these first-century Christians conspired to concoct the story of the resurrection and then were willing to endure persecution and death to protect their ruse.) By normal standards of evaluating historical events, eyewitness testimony, even of a non-impartial witness, is sufficient to confirm an event. But, for the sake of argument, let's concede to the critics and look in history for an objective source.

The Jewish historian Flavius Josephus (ca. A.D. 37–100) is universally recognized as one of the most reliable sources of information from the first century. Here is what this non-Christian reporter had to say about Jesus Christ in his *Antiquities of the Jews*:

Now there was about this time Jesus, a wise man, if it be lawful to call him a man, for he was a doer of wonderful works, a teacher of such men as receive the truth with pleasure. He drew over to him both many of the Jews, and many of the Gentiles. He was the Christ, and when Pilate, at the suggestion of the principal men among us, had condemned him to the cross, those that loved him at the first did not forsake him, for he appeared to them alive again the third day; as the divine prophets had foretold these and ten thousand other wonderful things concerning him. And the tribe of Christians so named from him are not extinct at this day.

...And So Will You (15:12-34)

After presenting evidence that verifies the reality of the resurrection, Paul uses that foundation to prove that every Christian will have a resurrected body too. The steps in his logical argument go like this:

- Without the resurrection of Christ, our faith would be futile.

- But we know that Christ actually rose from the dead, and that means that Christians will experience a resurrection as well.

- Just as the consequence of eternal death came into the world through the acts of one man (Adam), the means of eternal life is available through one man (Christ).

Paul then gives an abridged overview of the events that will happen when life as we know it comes to an end

(15:24-28). His summary of the "end times" events outlines how the resurrected Christ will eventually defeat forever the powers of Satan and the sting of death. That process began with Christ's resurrection, but it won't all fall into place until He returns to earth again.

But enough for looking into the future. Paul quickly brings his discussion back to the here and now. What does the reality of his resurrection mean to him now? Does it impact his everyday life? Of course it does! The certainty of the resurrection motivates him to engage in missionary ministries that put his life at risk. Knowing the Gospel to be true, he has little regard for the safety and comfort of his present life because he knows that an eternal, resurrected life awaits him. What about you? Does the reality of the resurrection affect your perspective on serving God?

*R*estoration or *R*esurrection?

Christ's resurrection (and your future one) must be contrasted with instances reported in the Bible when a person was restored to life. Several such miracles are mentioned: Elijah brought the son of the widow of Zarephath back to life (1 Kings 17:17-24), Jesus restored life back to the daughter of Jairus (Matthew 9:18-26) and to Lazarus (John 11), and when Peter prayed for a dead woman named Tabitha, she opened her eyes and sat up (Acts 9:36-43).

But these *restorations* are different from Christ's *resurrection*: Every one of the people who were restored to life eventually died again.

Resurrection, on the other hand, is more powerful than death. Christ lives for eternity (Hebrews 7:24), and the same will be true for you. Christ's resurrection to an eternal life is your guarantee of an eternal life (1 Corinthians 15:20).

A New and Improved Resurrection Body (15:35-58)

Some skeptics have doubted the reality of the resurrection because they cannot comprehend how it would work. Paul scoffs at this reasoning. After all, no one quite understands how a tree grows from a seed that is planted in the ground and dies. Yet no one doubts the reality of the vegetation that covers the earth.

Many mysteries remain about what our resurrected bodies will look like. Will we be recognizable to each other? What will be the apparent age of our appearance (will we look like we did when we died physically, or will we all look like we're in our mid-thirties)? Will be we able to fly? Paul doesn't tell us much, but he does give the Corinthians a few clues (which may have been all that he knew):

- We will each have a body.

- But it won't be a flesh and blood (earthly) body.

- Our resurrected bodies will have a spiritual dimension to them.

- Our earthly bodies are corruptible and subject to decay, but our new resurrected bodies will be immortal and incorruptible.

In this mini-treatise on the resurrection, Paul deflated the three prevailing philosophies that were unsettling the Corinthians:

- *Epicureanism* said that nothing existed beyond death. Paul said that we will live for eternity in our resurrected bodies.

- *Stoicism* said that the human soul merged with the deities upon death. Paul said that we will have resurrected bodies just as Christ had a resurrected body.

- *Platonism* said that only the soul is immortal, and we will have no body after death. Paul said that our physical bodies will die—only to be subsequently resurrected into spiritual bodies.

All of a sudden, death doesn't seem so bad, does it?

Final Instructions and Tentative Plans (16:1-24)

After his triumphant "How we thank God, who gives us victory over sin and death through Jesus Christ our Lord!" (15:57), you might think Paul would close his letter on a high note. But he doesn't. What follows is a bit anticlimactic, but it follows the pattern of Paul's other letters of closing with personal notes and comments.

Paul has a final instruction for them on a practical matter: the donation of money for the Christians in Jerusalem. Of all of those fledgling first-century churches, the Christians in Jerusalem were probably having the hardest time of it. Their poverty was so severe that some of the other churches were pitching in with financial help. Paul tells the Corinthians that they should be a part of this relief effort. He obviously knows them well enough to anticipate that they'll neglect this responsibility unless they implement the discipline of making weekly contributions.

Paul then adds some personal notes and comments about others:

- He gives them his future travel itinerary, which includes plans to make another visit to Corinth.

- He's sending Timothy (who will deliver the 1 Corinthians letter), and he wants them to treat him well.

- He makes reference to other people who have been instrumental in his ministry and in the life of the Corinthian church.

Intertwined in these rather mundane comments is a sense of his genuine affection for the Corinthian believers. He isn't ending this letter on a harsh note. Just the opposite. He keeps coming back to words of encouragement in his closing paragraphs:

- So, my dear brothers and sisters, be strong and steady, always enthusiastic about the Lord's work (15:58).

- Be on guard. Stand true to what you believe. Be courageous. Be strong. And everything you do must be done with love (16:13-14).

This letter has been tough for Paul to write. And it was probably tough for the Corinthians to read. But even though he has spoken severely to them, the Corinthians are his dear friends for whom he would sacrifice himself. He is most sincere as he closes his letter by saying, "My love to all of you in Christ Jesus" (16:24).

■ ■ ■

Study the Word

1. Using your own words, explain the Gospel message.

2. What would be the significance if Christ did *not* rise from the dead? What would be the impact to the Christian faith? What would be the impact to you personally?

3. Why is it such a big deal for Paul that the Corinthians understand that they too will have resurrected bodies?

4. Describe our future resurrected bodies. What are some of the things about those resurrected bodies that God has not yet revealed to us?

5. What principles can we learn from Paul's challenge for the Corinthians to support the poor Christians in Jerusalem? What is the relevance to you?

Chapter 10

More than any other epistle of Paul, 2 Corinthians allows us a glimpse into his inner feelings about himself, about his apostolic ministry, and about his relation to the churches which he founded and nurtured. This epistle is autobiographical in tone, then, though not in framework or substance.

Robert H. Gundry

A Change of Perspective

As we told you at the outset, the Corinthian letters are excellent resources to help you find your unique place in God's plan. No, you won't find the answer to what specific career or ministry you should pursue, and you won't find details about the time frame or place of your service. But 1 and 2 Corinthians contain clear guidelines for the actions and attitudes that you should have as you serve Christ.

From Paul's instructions in 1 Corinthians, you have learned several lessons:

- Serving God begins with turning away from the world's mentality and learning to think as God thinks.

- Ministry should direct the focus and glory to God, not yourself.

- You have been given spiritual gifts that will allow you to serve Him with supernatural results.

- Love is the overriding principle in the use of your spiritual gifts.

- The reality of the resurrection should motivate you to serve Christ regardless of the difficulties.

Now, as we move to 2 Corinthians, you won't be learning as much from the mistakes of the Corinthians. In this subsequent letter, Paul is much more reflective and introspective. Paul examines his own life and approach to ministry. As he recounts the things that he has learned, consider what you can apply to your own life.

God Will
Get You Through

2 Corinthians 1–3

*A*s you start reading 2 Corinthians, you are sure to notice a change in Paul's tone. It is softer, more conciliatory, and at times even apologetic. This attitudinal shift makes sense when you consider the events that transpired between the writing of 1 Corinthians and 2 Corinthians:

- Paul's protégé, Timothy, hand-delivered 1 Corinthians. The church's reaction to it was mixed. Some of Paul's adversaries used it as an opportunity to raise more criticisms against him. For the most part, however, the Corinthians received his corrections and challenges, and they set about to change their behavior as Paul had instructed.

- But any changes were apparently short-lived and less than wholehearted. To address worsening spiritual problems and a deteriorating relationship with the Corinthians, Paul made an emergency trip to Corinth. Things didn't go well on this "painful visit" (2:1). The friction was exacerbated by some insurgents who tried to elevate the anti-Paul sentiment in Corinth.

- Upon leaving Corinth, Paul wrote a brief but harsh letter to the Corinthians (7:8,12) that Titus hand delivered.

- Later, Titus linked back up with Paul in Macedonia and reported that the Corinthian church had responded well to the letter (7:13-16).

Now it is time for some follow-up correspondence. Paul deals with some lingering problems in 2 Corinthians, but for the most part he reflects on his challenging relationship with the Corinthians. Resisting an "I told you so" attitude, Paul uses the opportunity to share honestly about the strengths and weaknesses in his ministry as a means of encouraging the Corinthians in their faith.

Ever-Present Comfort (1:1-24)

Paul begins this letter with his standard greeting format, but this one is more abbreviated than the salutations in his other letters. Both he and his readers would understand the significance of identifying himself as "appointed by God to be an apostle of Christ Jesus" (1:1). These words reassured Paul of his calling in the face of criticism. They reminded the Corinthians of the authority that his words carried.

Paul moves promptly into an expression of thankfulness to God for being an ever-present comfort in the midst of difficult situations. Paul wasn't shy to emphasize the fact that he had endured hardships in his ministry. Look at the number of times in 1:3-7 that he uses words like "troubles" and "suffer." But also notice that words like "comfort" are used just as frequently to show that God is present when the going gets tough.

Knowing that the Corinthians would be curious to hear why he didn't visit them as he might have indicated in "the painful letter," Paul gives them a rundown on what his life has been like since his last visit. Although he doesn't get into specifics, he makes them aware that his missionary activities involve mortal danger at every turn. And he admits his human frailties in all of this. Without God's strength, he would have been overwhelmed. Apparently it helps to know that you're supported by a God who can raise the dead. (Uplifting the overwhelmed shouldn't be a problem for Him.) The prayers of encouraging Christians are a spiritual lift too.

Now Paul is ready to address the question of his integrity. Perhaps he wants to deal with this at the beginning of the letter so he can dispense with it and get to other subjects. Even though the "painful visit" had gone badly, the Corinthians expected that he would visit them again after a brief stay in Macedonia. Paul had indicated as much to them (and they might have eagerly anticipated his promised visit in light of the fact that they had responded well to the "painful letter"). But he stayed in Macedonia longer than he had expected, and he didn't visit Corinth as he had promised. Did this breach of his pledge indicate a lack of integrity (as his detractors suggested)? Paul knew this question was on their minds, so he dealt with it in this fashion:

- Christ and the Christian message are without duplicity. Paul doesn't say things that he doesn't mean.

- He has at all times acted with integrity, and they know that his track record proves this.

- Since he has proven himself trustworthy in the important aspects of life (such as the delivery of the Gospel message), doesn't it follow that he'd be trustworthy in the minor details of life (like a travel itinerary)?

- Moreover, he had subsequently changed his travel plans for *their* benefit. He didn't want to go through another painful visit that might damage and discourage them.

For Them or Him?

The passage of 1:3-11 is almost poetic in its description of God's continuing care and comfort. Do you think Paul wrote this to encourage the Corinthians to appreciate this aspect of God's nature? Or do you think he was saying these things because he needed to remind himself of God's presence as he undertook dealing with these rather immature Corinthians again?

Tough Love (2:1-17)

Sometime in your service for Christ, you may have to say difficult words to someone who needs to hear them. You won't be popular, but popularity isn't important to Christ. What's more important is that you care enough for your spiritual brothers and sisters to confront errant behavior and beliefs when necessary. This is the situation that Paul frequently faced in his relationship with the Corinthians. The passage of 2:1-4 reveals the attitude that we should have in such situations:

- Paul was not anxious to speak severely. He did not prefer to speak words of rebuke.

- But when he had to do it, he did so in love. His purpose was never to cause pain; he always desired correction and restoration.

- He never attempted to make people see things "his way." He encouraged people to see things God's way.

A great example of Paul's approach is revealed in 2:5-11. This passage deals with mending relationships with a person who had been disciplined in the church. A minority of scholars assumes that the individual in question is the member of the church who was sexually involved with his stepmother (whom Paul said should be cut off from the church in 1 Corinthians 5:1-5). The majority of scholars believe Paul is referring to a situation in which he had to deal harshly with one of his major critics in Corinth. Paul confronted the troublemaker and pointed out how his bitterness and divisive spirit was hurting the church, and the rest of the church realized that Paul was correct and joined in the disciplinary process. The majority view makes more sense. In the case of immorality, the person was wrong, knew he was wrong, and was unrepentant; thus, the church's only recourse was to cut him off from all church relationships. But in this passage, the person was evidently wrong but unaware of his error until the church discipline worked its intended result. The revealing aspect of this passage, once again, is Paul's response. We can learn a lot about how to respond in similar situations:

- Paul didn't take the matter personally. The dispute was directly about Paul, but he didn't let feelings of jealousy, pride, or humiliation prevent him from being loving or forgiving.

- Paul's clear motive was restoration and reconciliation, not retaliation.

- Paul cautioned that the discipline should not be inordinate. Once the corrective measures had achieved the desired purpose (which they had in this case), the church should offer full forgiveness and restoration.

Although Paul was interested in the restoration of this single individual, the spiritual condition of all of the Corinthian Christians was continually on Paul's mind. That's why Paul couldn't sit still in Troas while waiting for a report from Titus. Paul was so anxious to hear how the Corinthians were doing, he left Troas and met up with Titus in Macedonia. That's when Paul got the "things are going much better" report, so he moves into celebratory language about the sweetness of ministry as he reflects on this scenario in 2:12-17.

The New Covenant Transformation (3:1-18)

Strangers entering a community in the first century would customarily carry a letter of recommendation. Paul doesn't need such a letter because the Corinthian Christians are the best commendation of his ministry. He acknowledges that letters of reference are just words on paper, but the real proof of the effectiveness of his ministry is reflected in the lives and hearts of real people.

Paul states that he, along with all Christians, is an ambassador of the "new covenant." He characterizes the "old covenant":

- It brings death and condemnation.
- It was engraved on stone.
- Its glory fades.

He contrasts this with the "new covenant":

- It brings righteousness.
- It is of the Spirit and written on the hearts of people.
- It has a brighter, everlasting glory.

To be sure, the new covenant is better than the old one, but should Paul speak in such derogatory terms about the old covenant, which was instituted by God? Was he being critical of God's prior system? No—the fault of the old covenant was not with God but with humanity. Humankind was not able to live up to God's perfect standard due to sin, and the sin of humanity resulted in death. But the new covenant, which establishes a direct link between God and humankind through the death of Christ, is better because it brings righteousness to those who believe in Christ. Believers now have God's Holy Spirit indwelling them, and they don't have to refer to stone tablets to determine right from wrong. Humanity broke the old covenant, but God graciously provided a new covenant that depends upon Christ rather than upon us. That's what makes the new covenant so much better.

The references to the "veil" can be confusing unless you are familiar with the story of Moses from Exodus 34:29-35. After speaking with God, Moses' face shone with the reflected glory of God. Moses let the people of Israel see this radiated glory as he spoke the words of God to them, but otherwise he wore a veil over his face. Paul makes several points with analogies to the veil of Moses:

- Moses wore the veil so that people wouldn't notice God's glory fading from him. Thus it was a glory that was fading like the glory of the old covenant, which was going to be surpassed by the new covenant. The covenant that Moses explained was good, but the covenant that came through Jesus' death on the cross was perfect.

- In a sense, the Jews were living behind a veil. It obscured their view of God's plan and Christ's role in it. They weren't seeing the real meaning of Scripture.

Fortunately for Christians, God has lifted the veil from us. We can not only see God's glory but actually reflect it. We should be as mirrors that brightly reflect His glory, and we should be shining brighter as we become more and more like Him (3:18).

What Kind of Letter Are You?

Paul considered the Corinthians to be his "letter of recommendation." We too are "letters of recommendation," not for Paul, but for Jesus Christ. Everything we do and say reflects on Christ if we call ourselves Christians. When people see the substance of your life, do they think favorably about Christ?

■ ■ ■

Study the Word

1. Paul doesn't try to hide the fact that life can be difficult for a Christian. Why do you think God allows difficulties to happen?

2. Explain the drawbacks of the old covenant and the benefits of the new covenant.

3. Role play. Assume you are a critic of Paul's in the church at Corinth. Make an argument for why the church shouldn't trust him. Next, pretend that you are one of Paul's supporters in the church, and argue why the church should respect his authority.

4. Enumerate some of the principles you have learned about church discipline and the attitude you should have if you need to correct another believer.

5. Mention some specific, tangible ways in which a Christian can reflect the glory of God. How have you personally done so?

Chapter 11

In this passage, Paul the apostle gave another important outlook on his ministry. Outwardly, his life was not much to look at. He lived with suffering and hardship throughout his Christian experience. He was not very successful in human terms. At the same time, Paul remained confident of his high calling as an apostle of Christ by looking beyond his outward circumstances to his inward renewal in Christ's blessings and the great future that would be his when Christ returned. As we face suffering for the sake of the gospel, we can take courage in the same work of Christ within us.

Richard L. Pratt Jr.

A Job Title

Wouldn't God's will for your life be much easier to find if God simply told you what He wanted you to do? You are probably ready, willing, and anxious to start serving Him—if He'd just tell you your assignment. And if He won't tell you the specifics, at least a few clues would be nice—like the job title that accompanies your mission.

Well, stop your fretting. In the passage that you're about to read, Paul tells you the job title that is associated with the role Christ has in mind for you. We won't keep you in suspense any longer: God intends for you to a be an agent of reconciliation. That is the role in which God wants you to use your unique gifting, personality, and circumstances.

Now we suppose that you want the job description of an agent of reconciliation. That would be a good reason to keep reading.

Agents of Reconciliation

2 Corinthians 4–7

*W*hen we left off at the end of 2 Corinthians 3, Paul had just explained the concepts of living under the new covenant and reflecting—on an increasing basis— the glory of Christ. Now he is ready to explain that every Christian is a minister of the new covenant, and he uses the highs and lows from his own life to illustrate his points.

Frailties Are Good Things (4:1-18)

Presenting the new covenant to people is a wonderful ministry, but it is not easy. Despite the difficulties, Paul doesn't give up (4:1), and he doesn't want the Corinthians to be quitters either (4:16).

To illustrate the congruity of the *privilege* of ministry with the *problems* of ministry, Paul uses the metaphor of treasure in a clay jar. This illustration has several layers of meaning:

- *Treasure:* The treasure to which Paul refers is the new covenant. Paul ascribes the utmost value to "the brightness of the glory of God that is seen in the face of Jesus Christ" (4:6).

- *Clay Jars:* The jars of clay (4:7 NIV) are the Christians who carry the message of the new covenant. Just as now, people in the first century would not have put anything expensive in an inferior container. The Corinthians would have used boxes made of gold, silver, or ivory for their valuables. Paul must have caught their attention when he talked about putting something precious in an inexpensive clay pot. But that is exactly what God has done by entrusting the priceless Gospel message to Christians with all our physical, mental, emotional, and spiritual frailties.

God's design for this "precious treasure" in "perishable containers" is simply this: The power of God is revealed. Humans don't deserve any credit, adulation, or attention, Paul says; God is the one who deserves the glory. We are just wimps and weaklings, but God's strength gets us up and moves us onward. Here is how Paul lyrically presents this truth:

Because we are weak, we become...	*But because of God's strength, we...*
pressured by our troubles	are not crushed
perplexed	do not give up
hunted down	are not abandoned by God
knocked down	get back up and keep going

Paul had a great understanding of the relationship between our problems and God's purposes. In comparison, our troubles are trivial. When we have that perspective, we can look past the short-term difficulties and on to the long-term reward of God's glory. Thus, the things we can see in the present (our problems) are "quite small" when compared to what we can't yet see in the future (our eternal joy).

Cheap Pots

A Corinthian woman would not have placed any importance on a clay pot. They were cheap and ugly (the pots, not the Corinthian women). Fancy containers might have been displayed on a shelf, but clay pots were kept out of sight.

And so, in our service to Christ, our desire should not be to be on display and admired by others. Christ is the treasure. He should be the One who garners everyone's attention. Meanwhile, we can be in the cabinet under the sink with the rest of the utilitarian supplies.

A Transformed Life (5:1-21)

Paul shifts from housewares to a housing analogy. He says that our earthly bodies are like tents, makeshift and temporary. But in heaven, our bodies will have a "home" constructed by God. Thus begin Paul's initial thought processes about the nature of our transformed lives as Christians:

- We need not fear the end of our earthly existence. We can look forward to it because we'll be with the Lord.

- Our present bodies may have aches and pains, but that doesn't mean we want to die so we can be free of bodies altogether. We are excited about the future because we will have new bodies.

- God has given us a guarantee of the new life to come. The presence of the Holy Spirit in our lives right now is our guarantee of the things to come.

Paul keeps us in touch with reality. Being on earth now is difficult because we aren't yet with the Lord. That time will come, but even that won't be all fun and games. Christ will judge our service to Him. Thus our earthly experience is not a waste. It is preparation for eternity.

The somber expectation of standing at the Judgment Seat of Christ serves as our motivation. Paul is not overcome with fear and trembling, worrying about how Christ will evaluate his service. Instead, filled with reverence and awe for Christ, Paul wants to be judged to have been a good and faithful servant. Although he cares about the Corinthians, Paul isn't primarily concerned about their evaluation of the eternal significance of his work. His highest goal is to bring glory to God, and he works for the benefit of the Corinthians' spiritual welfare to accomplish that goal (5:13).

With that as the backdrop, now Paul lays out the job assignment that God has given to each and every Christian:

> *And God has given to us the task of reconciling people to him* (5:18).

As agents of reconciliation, we have two tasks:

- First, we must reconcile people to God. This isn't an onerous task. We have a wonderful message to bring to the world: "Through the work of Christ, God isn't going to hold your sins against you."

- But once people receive that message, our mission is not over. We have the subsequent assignment of helping immature Christians reconcile their conduct with the reality of their new and transformed life.

From what Paul says in 6:16-17, we know that our work of reconciliation shouldn't be accomplished with finger-pointing, browbeating, and humiliation tactics. Our work isn't about evaluating sin, immorality, and carnality. Our efforts should reflect the hope of the transformed life, which is the treasure of the Christian.

Love in Action (6:1-18)

As an agent of reconciliation, you can't let your own life get in the way of people seeing Jesus. This principle is double-barreled: (1) Don't distract them from Jesus, and (2) don't give them an opportunity to find fault with you.

> We try to live in such a way that no one will be hindered from finding the Lord by the way we act, and so no one can find fault with our ministry (6:3).

If you think this may put a crimp in your lifestyle, you are correct. This approach certainly put Paul through the wringer, and he enumerates specific examples of problems he has endured (6:4-5). Some situations in this list are just parts of life. But most of Paul's tough times were direct results of his service to Christ and engagement in the reconciliation process.

As difficult as the reconciliation process was, with all of the hardships that accompanied it, Paul never lost sight of the ultimate fact: He was serving God (6:8). With that reality in Paul's mind, he could continue whether things went well or not (and in 6:8-10, Paul gives another litany of examples from both ends of the spectrum).

One of the more difficult challenges of his ministry was dealing with the church in Corinth. But Paul sees that as one of the greatest examples of reconciliation. His references in 6:11-13 make that clear. In his attempts to reconcile the Corinthians back to God, he had made some harsh reprimands. But his loving spirit, and theirs, healed a once-fractured relationship, and by the time Paul wrote 2 Corinthians, he felt reconciled with them.

Unequally Yoked

The passage of 6:14-18 seems to be a diversion, but the subject may have been on Paul's mind because he was thinking about the tough times that a Christian endures. Why make matters worse than they need to be? Maybe this is why he inserts a warning on the dangers of associating with unbelievers in certain kinds of relationships. Certainly, Paul is not suggesting that a Christian cut off all relationships with the unsaved world. (He has already discharged this erroneous view in 1 Corinthians 5:9-11.) Here he is cautioning against situations in which a believer and a nonbeliever share a binding commitment that cannot be easily terminated.

Paul gives the analogy of two incompatible animals being yoked together. His readers would have known that a mule and an ox wouldn't be hitched together because their natures were mismatched. Similarly, whether in a marriage or certain business relationships, the perspectives of a Christian will be so opposite to those of an unbeliever with a worldly outlook that the two people will be unable to pull in the same direction.

Love's Payoff (7:1-16)

When you think about the hardships Paul endured to be an agent of reconciliation, you might wonder whether our mission is worth the hassle. In 2 Corinthians 7, Paul answers that question: No doubt about it. But Paul doesn't speak of the rewards of a reconciliation ministry in generic terms. He talks very pointedly about the joy he experienced in witnessing the transformed lives of the Corinthians. These were examples that the Corinthians could easily understand (and so can you now that you are one well-studied in the Corinthian experience).

To Paul's way of thinking, the sorrows of reconciliation are far outweighed by the spiritual joys that reconciliation brings. He gives some examples:

- *A painful visit and a pleasant response (7:5-7):* Paul was distraught after his painful visit and after sending his painful letter to the Corinthians. He did and said what was necessary, but it wasn't pleasant. But then Titus brought the report that the Corinthians had responded well. Did the result justify the difficult process? Judge for yourself from what Paul says:

    > When he told me how much you were looking forward to my visit, and how sorry you were about what had happened, and how loyal your love is for me, I was filled with joy! (7:7).

- *A stern letter and godly sorrow (7:8-12):* Paul would have preferred to avoid his stern and painful letter, but it was necessary to bring the Corinthians to a point of grief and conviction. The change in the Corinthians' lives was worth the stern letter and the sorrow they felt.

- *A rough road and restored relationships (7:13-16):* The outcome of the entire painful process has been encouraging to Paul. And through it Titus became a fan of the Corinthians.

Think for a moment about the chronology of Paul's relationships with the Corinthians. During his two previous visits and three previous letters, Paul dealt with them like a father dealing with a wayward teenage child. But Paul never waivered from the difficult assignment of being an agent of reconciliation to the Corinthians. And you've got to believe that he is thrilled with the results that God has brought about in the lives of the Corinthians. Why else would he say, "I have complete confidence in you" (7:16)?

■ ■ ■

$\mathcal{S}$tudy the $\mathcal{W}$ord

1. Can you think of (and explain) a different metaphor to illustrate Paul's "treasure in earthen vessel" point?

2. What keeps a Christian going when times are tough?

3. What is an agent of reconciliation?

4. Explain Paul's caution against being "unequally yoked" (6:14 KJV). Do you agree? Give some specific instances to which this principle applies.

5. Describe what you consider to be any benefits of suffering. Do you reap those benefits even if you brought about the consequences through your own doing? Is the pain difficult or less difficult to endure when someone else causes it?

*C*hapter 12

The New Testament does not teach us simply to give away possessions for the sake of giving them away or appearing virtuous. Nor does it encourage us to adopt a "simple lifestyle" because simplicity has merit in itself. Rather, all of these commands are put in the context of glorifying God and furthering the work of His kingdom, and of laying up treasures in heaven and increasing our heavenly reward.

Wayne Grudem

Money Is Not the Point

Many people consider the two chapters of 2 Corinthians 8–9 as the Bible's best teaching on the principles of financial stewardship. (In this sense, *stewardship* is Christianese for "how you handle your money.")

We'd venture a guess that you didn't think the subject of money would arise in a discussion of finding your place in God's plan. Well, it does, but not because money matters to God (because it doesn't). God already owns everything; He doesn't need your money (contrary to what many Christian fundraisers would have you believe). He can accomplish whatever He wants with or without money.

But God knows that money is important to you. And if you're sincerely interested in following His plan for your life, you must have an appropriate attitude about it.

Partnership in Ministry

2 Corinthians 8–9

*P*aul knew from the outset of writing 2 Corinthians that he was going to bring up the subject of collecting money for the Christians in Jerusalem. But he didn't lead with this request. He had to clear the air with the Corinthians on many issues before he got to the touchy subject of money. (Why are Christians hypersensitive about finances and giving?) So, throughout the first seven chapters of 2 Corinthians, Paul has patched things up and just finished on a high note as he talked about his complete confidence in the spiritual growth of the Corinthians. That is the condition (spiritual maturity) that is required to understand the principles of Christian stewardship, which happen to be contrary to our natural instincts.

A Prologue to Partnership (8:1-15)

Paul begins by inspiring the Corinthians with the example of what the Macedonian Christians gave to the church in Jerusalem. Perhaps Paul was after more than just inspiration; he might have been appealing to their competitive spirit as well. (Greece was divided into two major regions at the time. Corinth was in the southern region of Achaia; Macedonia was the northern region. A bit of rivalry existed between these two regions.) Using the Macedonian Christians as godly examples of spiritual generosity would certainly capture the attention of the Corinthians.

Paul was writing from Macedonia (2:13; 7:5), so the Corinthians knew that he was speaking from firsthand knowledge. He mentions the Macedonians' poverty and hardships, but then he brags that they have come to understand some of the dynamics of financial stewardship:

- Their generosity was rooted in their desire to know and follow God's will (8:5). They didn't make financial decisions on their own; they wanted God's direction in the matter.

- Their level of giving was not determined by calculating what was left after allowing for their own comfort and provisions. They gave more than they could afford (8:3).

- Paul didn't have to beg or pry contributions from them. They gave of their own free will (8:3).

With this spirit of generosity, the Macedonians considered sharing their finances with the Jerusalem Christians a "gracious privilege" (8:4).

Knowing that the Corinthians must have been pleased with their spiritual growth, Paul now puts giving into that context. He wants them to view stewardship with the same degree of importance as they have placed on other aspects of their faith (such as spiritual gifts). In fact, giving is a ministry (8:7). And it is a ministry that actually reflects the sincerity of our love for God. Lest they doubt this point, Paul cites the example of Jesus, who left the riches of His heavenly home to become poor so that we might inherit the treasure of a relationship with God and eternal life.

The Poverty of Christ

When on earth, Christ wasn't "poor" because He was raised by an impoverished carpenter or because as an adult He was a destitute, itinerant teacher. The poverty to which Paul refers is the fact that Christ set aside the right to exercise His divine powers and glory and, by so doing, humiliated Himself by becoming human.

About one year before Paul wrote 2 Corinthians, the Corinthians had begun to collect funds for the support of the impoverished and persecuted Christians in Jerusalem. In fact, Paul had earlier given them some suggestions about putting aside money on a weekly basis for this offering (1 Corinthians 16:1-4). But the Corinthians had apparently dropped the ball, and now Paul encourages them to revive their earlier efforts. Perhaps knowing that they might take the competition with the Macedonians to the extreme, Paul cautions them not to give so much that they jeopardize the support of their own families. Paul wants them to take a global, communal approach to giving. They weren't in a contest to see who could give the most. Rather, they should recognize that what we have belongs ultimately to God, and we should be willing to share among ourselves according to our respective needs.

But What Was the Amount?

We're sure that the competitive Corinthians were curious to know the amount of money that the Macedonians had contributed to the support of the church in Jerusalem. But Paul doesn't mention an amount. To his way of thinking—and to God's—the amount of money was not important. Their willingness to make themselves and their resources available to God was what counted.

Some Precautions for Partnership (8:16-24)

Paul had already endured some unjust personal criticism for allegedly using ministry as a guise to get rich. None of this was true, but it nonetheless was damaging to his reputation. And the reputation of a Christian always reflects on the reputation of Christ in the eyes of unbelievers and immature Christians. And that's what Paul is worried about. He doesn't want anyone to have questions about the financial integrity of the offering collected for the saints in Jerusalem

With guidelines that are instructive for churches and ministries of today, Paul reveals that he has implemented a plan of fiscal accountability for the Jerusalem offering. A delegation of men will be responsible for it. One of the group will be Titus, who was well-known to the Corinthians. But everyone knew that Titus was a protégé of Paul, which could be an issue if some suspected Paul's integrity and Titus' loyalty to him. To assure that adequate safeguards existed, Paul says that two other respected Christian men would travel with Titus to assure proper handling of the funds and delivery of the offering in Jerusalem.

The principles in this passage are very relevant to churches and ministries of this generation. The cause of Christ has suffered embarrassment by numerous financial scandals. But not only mega organizations are to blame. Many individual Christians have displayed financial irresponsibility to the detriment of their business associates. Paul's remedy to these situations is simple:

- We should honor the Lord by displaying integrity in our financial affairs, whether as a church, a ministry, or as individuals.

- If we are operating with donated funds, then we have a responsibility to make sufficient financial disclosures to avoid suspicion of impropriety.

*I*t's *M*ore than *G*iving— *I*t's *P*artnership!

Paul's teaching in 2 Corinthians 8–9 is often described as principles for giving. Although "giving" is a commonly used term among twenty-first-century Christians, it is not as precise as Paul would want. Paul uses two terms in this passage almost interchangeably. Sometimes he uses "give" (which in the Greek language is *doron*). But more often he uses the Greek term *koinonia,* which conveys the concept of "partnership." Does that term alter your understanding of what Paul intended when he spoke of "giving"?

The Preparation for Partnership (9:1-5)

If you didn't know better, you'd think that Paul was an attorney. Look at how he can work both sides of a situation. Earlier, he used the actions of the Macedonians to inspire the Corinthians in their giving (8:1-5). Now he explains that he has already told the Macedonians about the generosity of the Corinthians (and that they've been collecting an offering for Jerusalem for more than a year). He used each group to be an encouragement for the other.

Paul hopes that he hasn't boasted about the Corinthians prematurely. He knows they have good intentions, but he also knows that they've lapsed in their fundraising intensity. So he is sending the delegation of Titus and the others to help them complete the task.

This passage shows us the practicality of giving: It doesn't happen by itself. Oh sure, the Holy Spirit may sometimes prompt you to give spontaneously. But most of the time we need to be disciplined about it. It takes planning and persistence. By our nature, we are most likely to delay making a financial gift to the Lord's work. We should be aware of this fact and structure giving into our regular routine so that it is organized and systematic.

Paul knew the tendencies of the Corinthians, so he thought that Titus and the other two guys could help. But don't get the mistaken impression that these were three goons that Paul dispatched as "enforcers" for the purpose of collecting funds. On the contrary, Paul sent them to be "encouragers" to the Corinthians. But just so the Corinthians didn't get the wrong idea, Paul concludes this passage with, "I want it to be a willing gift, not one given under pressure" (9:5).

The Underlying Principles of Partnership (9:6-15)

Without a lot of fanfare, Paul articulates several very important principles for giving. They applied to the Corinthians' situation, but they apply to ours as well:

- Giving is an individual matter (9:7). No set figure applies equally to everyone.

- You should give only if you are anxious to do so. God loves a cheerful giver (9:7).

- Giving should never be the result of a targeted guilt trip or of arm twisting (9:7).

- You can't out-give God. Your needs won't go unmet if you give to others as God directs you to do. He will take care of your financial need (9:9).

- As you give, God will make you more generous (9:10).

- Your giving will bless others and cause them to grow in their relationship with God (9:11-12).

- You will grow spiritually as you learn to give. God will make you more generous, and your gifts will be a means by which you glorify God (9:10,13). And you will receive the benefit of the prayers of those who are grateful for your generosity toward them (9:14).

A few shrewd individuals figure that giving to God is a good way to make a fast buck. They heard that if you give to God, He'll give even more back to you. They're thinking that if they give $100, they're likely to get $1000 back. That's a good rate of return, but they haven't read the fine print in God's stewardship guarantee.

Here's the verse where some think they've found a loophole:

> *Yes, you will be enriched so that you can give even more generously* (9:11).

Notice what this verse says and what it doesn't say. First, it says that when you give to God, He will "enrich" you, but that doesn't necessarily mean in a financial way. Certainly the blessings from giving that Paul describes in 9:11-12 are of a spiritual nature, not a financial benefit. Second, the verse says that God's reciprocal blessings to you are for the purpose of allowing you to be of even more help to others. In God's system, you don't give so you can get. Rather, you give, and then God blesses you back, so you can give some more.

Will God Settle for a Flat Rate?

Giving should be motivated by love, not by some preset standard rate (like tipping in a restaurant). Under the Law of the Old Testament, the Jews were required to give 10 percent of the agricultural produce from their land to the support of the priests and Temple staff. (Every third year, they had to give an additional 10 percent for distribution to the indigent.) But we are obviously free from any arbitrary standard because no one is under pressure—or any requirement—to give. Does that mean that we can give less than 10 percent? Yes, if that is appropriate. Our love for Christ and for others should determine the proper amount, which means we may give more than 10 percent. Just ask yourself, "How much has Christ blessed me?" and let your answer be your guide.

■ ▨ ▣

Study the Word

1. This passage has been dealing with financial stewardship, but as Christians we are called to be stewards
   (responsible managers) of *all* that God has given to us,
   not just our finances. What has this passage taught you
   about stewardship of your other resources (such as
   your time, possession, and talents)?

2. In 2 Corinthians 8:15, Paul makes a reference to the
   Israelites collecting manna. Read that story in Exodus
   16. How does that story amplify the point Paul was
   trying to make?

3. This entire passage on financial stewardship involves raising money for believers in another city (Jerusalem). No part of the passage deals with the Corinthians collecting money for use in their own Christian community. Does this fact change your perspective of what giving is all about?

4. With all of the worthwhile ministries that could use financial support, how should you determine where to donate your money? How should you determine the appropriate amount to give?

5. List at least five principles about giving that you have learned from studying this passage.

Chapter 13

The difference in tone between [2 Corinthians] chapters 1–9 and 10–13 is easily explained by the change of focus from the repentant majority to the rebellious minority.... The opposition addressed in 10–13 apparently consisted of Jews who claimed to be apostles but who preached a false gospel and were enslaving in their leadership. Chapters 10–13 were written to expose these "deceitful workers" and defend Paul's God-given authority and ministry as an apostle of Jesus Christ.

Bruce Wilkinson and Kenneth Boa

A Little Bit More
You Need to Know

When you started this study 12 chapters ago, we told you that 1 and 2 Corinthians would provide you with insights about finding your unique place in God's plan. Just look at the guidelines that Paul has emphasized for your spiritual growth and service:

- Change the way you think from the world's mind-set to God's paradigm.

- Your lifestyle and behavior must be consistent with spiritual thinking.

- Sometimes you'll need to restrict your liberty out of love for someone else who isn't as spiritually mature.

- Christ should be the focal point of everything that you do, and nothing done in service or worship of Christ should draw attention to yourself.

- God has given you supernatural gifts of the Holy Spirit, but you should use them in love for the benefit of others and not for your personal glory.

- You can expect hardship and challenges in your Christian walk, but Christ is sufficient to meet your every need.

- Your overriding assignment is to be an agent of reconciliation, drawing people to God and helping them align their life with the reality of their new nature.

- On the practical side of everyday life, you must recognize your responsibility as a steward—to share with others what God has given to you.

But unfortunately, Paul includes one more lesson to learn. We say "unfortunately" because this lesson involves the appropriate way to respond to criticism from those who are supposed to be on your side.

Firm Convictions
Withstand Criticism

2 Corinthians 10–13

*W*ith the final four chapters of 2 Corinthians, we find a rather peculiar ending to Paul's letter. He seems to have finished his general comments to the Corinthian Christians at the end of chapter 9, and from this point forward he is speaking solely to his critics. We don't know exactly what attacks people have made against Paul, but we can deduce the issues from his responses.

You aren't likely to run into identical criticism as you minister for Christ. But we can almost guarantee you that ridicule and disparagement are in your future if you are sincerely and effectively working on Christ's behalf. Some of these attacks against you might come from non-Christians, but we are sorry to say that your obstacles and critics are more likely to be other Christians.

When others condemn your intentions and obedience to God—and they will—you've got to channel your tendency to react defensively. Here's the tricky part. You should defend your *message* (that is, what Christ has called you to do and say) more than the *messenger* (that is, you). This requires a fine balance.

Because the appropriate response to criticism is counterintuitive, we need a good example of how to handle these delicate situations. And that's exactly what Paul gives us in 2 Corinthians 10–13. These lessons will give you one more building block in the foundation of understanding your unique role in God's plan.

An Astute Use of Gentleness and Kindness (10:1-18)

Although we are reading only Paul's side of the conversation, we can infer that his critics have made specific personal attacks against him. To each one of these (which we've put in *italics* below), Paul had a well-reasoned response:

- *Paul can write a harsh and critical letter, but when he comes to Corinth in person, he wimps out—he's pathetic.* Paul says that he can speak boldly face-to-face, but he hopes that kind of confrontation won't ever be necessary (10:2).

- *Paul is operating from human motives.* Paul responds that God is the source of both his actions and his message. He is able to deflate and defeat worldly arguments for precisely that reason (10:3-5).

- *Just look at him. He is such an eyesore that he shouldn't assume a leadership role.* Paul zings them with a counterpunch that they are assessing spirituality on the shallow criteria of physical appearance (10:7).

- *Paul tries to be a big shot with all the churches in Greece and the outlying regions. Well, that might work elsewhere, but he doesn't have authority here in Corinth.* Paul reminds them that he was the one who brought the Gospel message to their region and established their church, but he has never taken credit for the ministry that others have contributed (10:14-15).

Paul's greatest argument appears to be his concession that "I wouldn't dare say that I am as wonderful as these other men who tell you how important they are!" (10:12). But the irony of this statement is readily apparent in the next sentence, where he says that they make the mistake of measuring their importance against each other. They should be comparing themselves to Christ (and then they wouldn't think they're so great). What a lesson for us. We might seem okay when we compare ourselves to the next guy, but we aren't striving for next-guy-likeness. If we're after Christlikeness, then Christ should be the one against whom we measure ourselves.

At the outset of this point-and-counterpoint banter, Paul mentions two words to describe the nature of his response to his critics. These words are tremendously instructive:

- *Gentleness:* The Greek word used by Paul, *prautes,* describes someone who is somewhere between "too angry" and "never angry at all." It is a word that suggests a person who has his anger under control and only gets angry at the right time for the right reasons. This lets us know that Paul was not over-reacting and not responding in vindictiveness or retaliation.

- *Kindness:* The Greek word used here, *epieikeia,* connotes justice that is softened by the circumstances. This is a perfect response for a Christian. We must always pursue justice, but our justice must always be tempered by love. And that is exactly the approach that Paul was using with his critics.

*W*hat *D*id *P*aul *L*ook *L*ike?

We don't know much about Paul's appearance except that he might not have been too easy to look at. About the only recorded description of him is found in a book called *The Acts of Paul and Thecla,* which was written about A.D. 200. By that account, Paul was "a man of little stature, thin-haired upon the head, crooked in the legs, of good state of body, with eyebrows meeting, and with nose somewhat hooked, full of grace, for sometimes he appeared like a man and sometimes he had the face of an angel."

I Don't Want to Say This, but I Will (11:1-33)

This passage is filled with things that Paul would rather not say—things about himself. Self-promotion by a Christian sickened Paul, and he knew that his critics used this tactic. As we have seen throughout 1 and 2 Corinthians, Paul preferred not to defend his dignity and authority. But now he was forced to do so because God's dignity and authority were coming into question.

Paul's critics viewed themselves as some sort of "super apostles." Paul acknowledges that they are better orators than he is, but he says that's all they've got. They don't know what they are talking about. Paul, on the other hand, may not be as easy to listen to, but he has continually proved that he speaks the truth (11:6).

Next, Paul addresses an issue that had been eating at the Corinthians. Paul had always refused to take money from them when he was in Corinth, but the Corinthians know that he accepted contributions from the church in Philippi. Was he playing favorites? Paul says no, and he makes an important distinction. Paul never accepted money from the Philippians while he was working in Philippi. Paul's policy was always to maintain financial independence from the churches where he was presently ministering. Only after he left Philippi did he receive (and accept) financial support from that church. The fact that Paul's critics in Corinth are making an issue of this situation proves that they are not well intentioned and that they are fake apostles who are trying to deceive the Corinthians (11:13).

Although he considers self-promotion distasteful and foolishness, Paul gives a little glimpse into his biography as an apostle. Without a doubt, he has endured a brutalized life for the sake of Christ (including beatings, imprisonments, and shipwrecks). He refrains from saying the obvious: The so-called "super apostles" of Corinth don't have this kind of history of service. Their only accomplishments have been to criticize someone who is actually involved in ministry.

*H*ere *C*omes the *B*ride

As with the previous chapter, the key to understanding Paul's attitude in this passage is found at the beginning of his argument. As much as he does not want to promote his own credentials, he explains that he is compelled to do so. To understand his illustration of a Jewish wedding, you've got to know some of the traditions:

- Just as our contemporary weddings include a best man and bridesmaids, every Jewish wedding involved two people called "friends of the bridegroom."

- They were responsible for many of the logistical details of the wedding festivities, but their most important job was to guarantee the chastity of the bride.

The New Testament often refers to Christ as the groom and the church as His bride. Paul views himself as a "friend of the bridegroom." As such, he is responsible to do whatever is necessary to guarantee the chastity of the bride, and that means he'll do things he doesn't like (such as listing his accomplishments as an apostle) in order to keep the Corinthian Christians from being seduced by fake apostles.

The same should be true for us. In our service to Christ, we may have to take a stand or be involved in situations that we would prefer to avoid. But our personal preferences should be irrelevant compared to the value of our sacred calling.

Pain: A Constant Reminder (12:1-21)

If Paul really wanted to brag (which he doesn't), he would tell the Corinthians about the spiritual visions he had 14 years earlier. Unfortunately for us, we don't know what Paul saw (and what he learned) when he was given a glimpse of Paradise because he keeps that matter private. But that is exactly the point. He is not trying to impress the Corinthians with the depth of his own spirituality.

Instead, he wants them drawn to the depths of truth in his teachings about God.

This is the only place in all of Scripture where you'll find a reference to Paul's visions. We can understand why he didn't go into detail about the experience with the Corinthians, but we wonder why he refrained from mentioning it in any of his other epistles. Maybe he gives us a clue in the next few verses, where he talks about his pride. Maybe Paul struggled with pride, and maybe that is why he was so resistant to "boasting" about his accomplishments (he didn't want to play into his weakness).

Paul says that God gave him a "thorn in his flesh" to keep him from getting proud. The last 20 centuries have seen quite a bit of speculation about exactly what Paul meant. Some interpreters have tried to spiritualize the meaning (suggesting "the thorn" referred to Paul's physical temptations or temptations to abandon his apostolic calling), but these interpretations seem to overlook the fact that pain was involved with this affliction. (The word that Paul used for "thorn" was *skolops*, which can also mean "stake.") Most commentators believe Paul's comments refer to a physical infirmity rather than a metaphysical problem. These are some of the more widely held interpretations for Paul's "thorn in the flesh":

- *His physical appearance.* Although being ugly might have been a slight hindrance in his ministry, it probably didn't involve pain.

- *Epilepsy.* But does this mean that the visions of Paradise that inspired him might have been epileptic-induced seizures?

- *Severe migraine headaches.*

- *Very poor eyesight or impaired vision.* This could have caused concomitant headaches.

But let's stop speculating about what we *don't* know and focus on what we *do* know about Paul's "thorn in the flesh." Here is where this passage gets particularly relevant to you. God intended Paul's affliction to make him all the more dependent upon God. It was a constant reminder to Paul that God was all-sufficient. From Paul's bio, we know that he found God all-sufficient in many circumstances:

- intense physical pain
- exhaustion
- resistance and conflict
- criticism and slander

And God is all-sufficient for your needs as well, whatever they may be. Aren't you glad you don't have to look to your own strength to carry you through the difficulties of life? You can relax in your weakness because God says to you, as He said to Paul:

> *My gracious favor is all you need. My power works best in your weakness* (12:9).

Don't Go to This Church

After mentioning his credentials, perhaps Paul worried that the Corinthians might think that he was worried about their opinion of him. Well, he makes clear that he isn't trying to ingratiate himself to them in the last part of 2 Corinthians 12. There he speaks boldly of what he is afraid he might find upon his next visit to Corinth. If you are ever looking for a church to attend, this list tells you the characteristics of an ungodly church. If you see an abundance of these traits in a church you are visiting, keep looking.

And in Closing—Four Things (13:1-14)

In many of Paul's letters, his closing passages are filled with personal comments and greetings to individuals. Not so here. Although Paul knows the Corinthians by name, he keeps his comments short and generic. Look for these four elements as you read this last chapter:

1. *A warning* (13:2): He doesn't want a showdown on his next visit, but he won't shy away from one. He will speak God's truth in the power of the Holy Spirit, and the fakes and phonies better take cover.

2. *A challenge* (13:5): Paul tells the Corinthians to take a spiritual audit of their lives. They have been playing around long enough. They need to determine whether their faith is genuine.

3. *A prayer* (13:7): Paul is praying that they will think right so they will live right. He prays that they will grow in spiritual maturity.

4. *A hope* (13:10): Paul's sincere hope is that he won't have to deal harshly with them on his next visit.

His final expressions seem to summarize all that he has said before. Think of these directions in the context of his earlier call for them to be agents of reconciliation (both to bring people to Christ and to reconcile their lifestyle with the reality of their new nature):

- Rejoice in the Lord.

- Change your ways.

- Encourage each other.

- Live in harmony and peace.

With this perspective and goal, they will experience God's presence. And that is what he has been working for all along.

Now, What About You?

We are a lot like the Corinthian Christians, don't you think? If you discount the fraudulent "apostles" in the group who were intentionally trying to misinform and mislead, the rest of them were Christians sincerely trying to follow God. Oh sure, they were distracted by pride and their culture, but their intent was to be good Christians and follow God's will. That description seems to fit most Christians living today.

Through his teachings, Paul tried to get the Corinthians to understand that they will experience exponential spiritual growth once they master the fundamentals of Christian living: to think like Christ, to act like Christ, and to be motivated by Christ.

And the same is true for you. Master those fundamentals, and you will realize your unique role in God's plan.

◻ ◻ ◻

Study the Word

1. Imagine that someone has unjustly criticized you for something you have done in the church. Using Paul as a model, how should you respond?

2. Do you have a "thorn in the flesh" that God hasn't taken away? What has it taught you about God?

3. In what circumstances is talking about the accomplishments of your ministry for Christ permissible? What guidelines should you keep in mind?

4. How can you determine who has authority in the church? How should a church handle opposing claims to leadership? What criteria did Paul suggest that the Corinthians use in evaluating him and the "super apostles"?

5. What does "examining yourself" mean? How do you do it? How often should you do it? What are you supposed to do when the assessment is finished?

Dig Deeper

*W*e like to write, but we really like to study. As with all of our books, we preceded the writing of this Bible study with many hours of study and research. We've come across many books that we found quite helpful and informative. Hoping that you'll want to proceed further in your study of 1 and 2 Corinthians, we'd like to recommend some books to you.

Commentaries

A great verse-by-verse commentary is the *Life Application Bible Commentary*. This set is written by the same team that designed and wrote the notes to the *Life Application Bible*. This is a multivolume set (and we used the one on 1 and 2 Corinthians).

William Barclay has an excellent commentary set in his Daily Study Bible Series. A single volume contains his comments on both 1 and 2 Corinthians. He takes a passage at a time (usually about 10 to 15 verses) and gives great background information to the text.

We also found the *Holman New Testament Commentary* (1 and 2 Corinthians volume written by Richard L. Pratt Jr.)

to be helpful. The general editor of this series is Max Anders, who has a well-deserved reputation for making Bible passages understandable.

Perhaps the easiest resource to read was the Corinthians volumes in the Thru The Bible Commentary Series. This set was taken from the *Thru The Bible* radio broadcasts of Dr. J. Vernon McGee. Nobody says it plainer than Dr. McGee.

Another commentary set is the John Phillips Commentary Series. It provides a detailed outline for every passage. (Separate volumes are available for 1 and 2 Corinthians.)

General Bible Study Helps

If you want an overview, then check out *Knowing God 101* and *Knowing the Bible 101*. More information about these books is on page 173.

We're always pulling *A Survey of the New Testament* by Dr. Robert H. Gundry off the shelf for background information.

Another one of our favorite Bible scholars is Dr. Lawrence O. Richards. His *Bible Teacher's Commentary* is excellent.

The Bible Knowledge Commentary includes an Old Testament volume and a New Testament volume (John F. Walvoord and Roy B. Zuck, general editors). These books will take you verse-by-verse through the entire Bible.

Bible Translations

You can't do any kind of Bible study without an actual Bible. Of course, that is obvious to everyone. What is often puzzling, however, is which Bible translation you should use. We recommend that your primary study Bible be a *literal* translation (as opposed to a paraphrase), such as the *New International Version* (NIV), or the *New American Standard Bible* (NASB). However, in your devotional reading, using a Bible paraphrase, such as The *Living Bible* or *The Message,* is perfectly acceptable.

The translation we used in this study on 1 and 2 Corinthians is the *New Living Translation* (NLT), a Bible translation that uses a method called "dynamic equivalence." This means that the scholars who translated the Bible from the original languages (Hebrew and Greek) used a "thought-for-thought" translation philosophy rather than a "word-for-word" approach. It's just as accurate but easier to read. In the final analysis, the Bible that's best for you is the Bible you enjoy reading because you can understand it.

A Word About Personal Pronouns

When we write about God, we prefer to capitalize all personal pronouns that refer to God, Jesus, and the Holy Spirit. These would include *He, Him, His*, and *Himself.* However, not all writers follow this practice, and nothing is wrong with that. In fact, personal pronouns for God were not capitalized in the original languages, which is why you'll find that many Bible versions use *he, him, his*, and *himself.*

Bruce and Stan would enjoy hearing from you. Contact them with your questions, comments, or to schedule them to speak at an event.

Twelve Two Media
P.O. Box 25997
Fresno, CA 93729-5997

E-mail: info@twelvetwomedia.com

Web site: www.twelvetwomedia.com

Exclusive Online Feature

Here's a Bible study feature you're really going to like! Simply go online at:

www.christianity101online.com

There you'll find a Web site designed exclusively for users of the Christianity 101 Bible Studies series. When you log on to the site, just click on the book you are studying, and you will discover additional information, resources, and helps, including...

- *Background Material*—We can't put everything in this Bible study, so this online section includes more material, such as historical, geographical, theological, and biographical information.

- *More Questions*—Do you need more questions for your Bible study? Here are additional questions for each chapter. Bible study leaders will find this especially helpful.

- *Answers to Your Questions*—Do you have a question about something in your Bible study? Post your question and an "online scholar" will respond.

- *FAQ's*—In this section are answers to some of the more frequently asked questions about the book you are studying.

What are you waiting for? Go online and become a part of the Christianity 101 community!

Christianity 101®

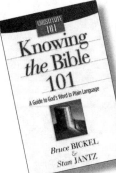

Knowing the Bible 101
Enrich your interaction with Scripture with this user-friendly guide, which shows you the Bible's story line and how each book fits into the whole. Learn about the Bible's themes, terms, and culture, and find out how you can apply the truths of every book of the Bible to your own life.

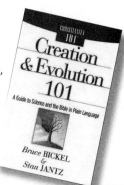

Creation & Evolution 101
With their distinctively winsome style, Bruce Bickel and Stan Jantz explore the essentials of creation and evolution and offer fascinating evidence of God's hand at work. Perfect for individual or group use.

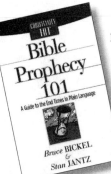

Bible Prophecy 101
In their contemporary, down-to-earth way, Bruce and Stan present the Bible's answers to your end-times questions. You will appreciate their helpful explanations of the rapture, the tribulation, the millennium, Christ's second coming, and other important topics.

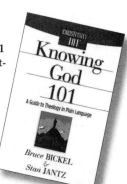

Knowing God 101
This book is brimming with joy! Whatever your background, you will love the inspiring descriptions of God's nature, personality, and activities. You will also find straightforward responses to the essential questions about God.